The farm wildlife handbook

Edited by Richard Winspear

Citation

For bibliographic purposes this book should be referred to as
Winspear R (ed.) (2007) *The farm wildlife handbook*.
The RSPB, Sandy.

The techniques described or referred to in this book do not necessarily reflect the policies of the RSPB or individuals involved in its production.

No responsibility can be accepted for any loss, damage or unsatisfactory results arising from the implementation of any of the recommendations within this book

The use of proprietory and commercial trade names in this handbook does not necessarily imply endorsement of the product by the authors or publishers.

Published by
The Royal Society for the Protection of Birds
The Lodge, Sandy, Bedfordshire SG19 2DL

Designed by
NatureBureau

Printed by
Information Press

10-digit ISBN 1 905601 11 5
13-digit ISBN 978 1 905601 11 0

Reviewers

Caroline Daguet	British Dragonfly Society	Chapter 10
Iain Diack	Natural England	Chapter 11
Richard Dodd	The Bat Conservation Trust	Chapter 4
Anne-Marie McDevitt	The RSPB (Northern Ireland)	all chapters
Mark O'Brien	The RSPB (Scotland)	Chapter 6
Nick Tomlinson	The Bat Conservation Trust	Chapter 4
Mike Williams	Environment Agency	Chapter 10

Contents

INTRODUCTION

This handbook pulls together conservation management advice for a wide range of farmland wildlife to enable the integration of the needs of wider biodiversity into a conservation plan. Collectively, the groups covered in this book represent species from the whole range of farmland habitats, and by managing for these, a much wider range of biodiversity will benefit. It is the first time that experts from so many wildlife interests have been brought together to compile one volume on farmland wildlife conservation.

Habitats of conservation importance on lowland farmland (such as semi-improved grassland and heathland) are generally very rare and planning their management requires careful consideration of many site-specific factors. These habitats are covered in detail in the literature listed below. Generic management of habitat features on lowland farmland (eg hedgerows, ditches and field margins) was covered in the companion volume *A management guide to birds of lowland farmland.*

The first chapter sets the scene for planning wildlife conservation. The subsequent chapters explain the management that benefits individual groups of conservation concern or agricultural importance, written by an expert on the subject. These chapters consist of an introduction to the group, a description of their conservation status and habitat requirements, and details of the management that will provide these requirements. These chapters provide an overview of the best management advice available. The references for further reading are given for those who want to study the detailed literature for individual species groups.

References for management of lowland farmland habitats of conservation significance:

Benstead P, Drake M, Jose P, Mountford O, Newbold C and Treweek J (1997) *The wet grassland guide: managing floodplain and coastal wet grasslands for wildlife.* The RSPB, Sandy.

British Trust for Conservation Volunteers on-line handbooks: http://handbooks.btcv.uk/handbooks/index

Crofts A and Jefferson R G (eds) (1999) *The lowland grassland management handbook.* 2nd edition. English Nature/The Wildlife Trusts, Peterborough.

Day J, Symes N and Robertson P (2003) *The scrub management handbook: guidance on the management of scrub on nature conservation sites.* FACT/English Nature, Peterborough.

RSPB, NRA and RSNC (1994) *The new rivers and wildlife handbook.* The RSPB, Sandy.

Symes N and Curry F (2005) *Woodland management for birds: a guide to managing for declining woodland birds in England.* The RSPB, Sandy.

Symes N C and Day J (2003) *A practical guide to the restoration and management of lowland heathland.* The RSPB, Sandy.

Winspear R and Davies G (2005) *A management guide to the birds of lowland farmland.* The RSPB, Sandy.

The Farm Wildlife website, www.farmwildlife.info, has case studies of farm wildlife conservation, a library of links to other websites with information on conservation management on farmland and a discussion forum to ask questions or post new ideas. Experts from many of the organisations involved in the production of this handbook also contribute to, and answer questions raised on this website.

PART 1
PLANNING FOR CONSERVATION ON FARMLAND

1 Planning for conservation on farmland

1.1 Priorities for farm wildlife conservation

Wildlife conservation can be a profitable part of a farm business, but the scale of implementation will often be constrained by resources somewhere along the line, be it the staff time, money out of the farmer's pocket or cost to the agri-environment scheme budget. It may not be possible to meet all of the conservation objectives on a farm. In general, created habitats rarely achieve the wildlife value of existing, long-established sites, and conserving what is already there is also a more cost-effective strategy. The following sets out the order of priority to maximise the value for the amount of effort or money spent.

1. Maintain existing wildlife habitats in good condition through continued good management.
2. Restore degraded habitats through changes in current management.
3. Create new wildlife habitats on land of little or no existing interest to expand or connect existing habitats, or to provide missing or scarce habitat requirements for important species found on or close to the farm.
4. Create new wildlife habitats on unproductive areas of the farm to add wildlife value to intensively managed farmland – a farm that only contains common habitats and species can still make a valuable contribution to wildlife conservation by creating and managing habitats to boost its wildlife value.

Whilst the priorities are to maintain or restore the quality of habitats and provide for the important species, more biodiversity will usually come with diversity of management at every level. In general, a mixed farming system will hold more biodiversity that a specialised farming system, a wide crop rotation will hold more biodiversity than a simple crop rotation and a habitat managed in a range of ways will hold more biodiversity than a habitat under one management regime.

In this handbook, you will see that ditches used by water voles are very different to ditches managed for breeding waders. Ditch management can only contribute to the conservation of both of these if different types of ditch are maintained on different parts of the site. Re-profiling ditches to make them accessible for wading birds will only be effective if carried out in open areas of suitable grassland for nesting. If such action would compromise the conservation of water voles, then alternative measures should be considered, such as creation of additional foot drains or wader scrapes.

It will not be possible to judge the ideal location and range of habitats required for all of the species on the farm, but the landscape character can help determine the best course of action. For example, it may be desirable to allow hedges to grow above 2 m tall and encourage hedgerow trees to become established on some areas of the farm. However, such action would be detrimental to some open farmland species, such as breeding waders. In planning where to allow hedgerows to grow up, it is more suitable to site them in wooded areas of the farm, especially if these hedges can connect patches of woodland, than in traditionally open areas of the farm where open farmland species may be resident. In general, wildlife habitats will have added value if they complement or connect areas of similar habitat.

1.2 Developing and implementing a conservation plan for the farm

There are four essential steps to developing and implementing a good conservation plan: gather existing information on the site, visit the site to evaluate the priorities and opportunities, develop the practical implementation necessary and explain the plan to everybody who needs to know about it. An adviser should involve the farmer in the development of the action plan, as the farmer's aspirations or concerns need to be considered when deciding the type or scale of changes to be made. Discussion of past and present farm management may also help evaluate the value and suitable management of some habitats, such as semi-improved grasslands. The four steps are detailed further in Box 1.1.

Box 1.1 Steps in the development of a conservation plan.

Step 1 Gathering information

- Consult the statutory agency to find out if there are any designated sites (eg SSSI's or ASSI's) on the farm, and whether there are specific priority species or habitats targetted by the agri-environment schemes
- Check whether any habitat survey has been conducted (eg a phase I habitat survey maps the broad habitat categories and will identify any semi-natural habitats that will need to be considered in a plan) – if not, aerial photographs may help make an initial habitat assessment
- Old maps and photographs may show past management, which may indicate the value or previous extent of some habitats
- Search for any species records held by conservation organisations or biological record centres on or within 2 km of the farm, which may be supported by conservation action

Step 2 Site visit

- Regardless of whether there is any existing information, a site visit is essential to map and assess the condition of habitats – spring or summer are the best seasons to survey many of the species groups, such as in-field plant composition, nesting birds and flying insects
- Ground truth the presence of important habitats on the farm
- Assess the quality of each habitat and categorise each as worthy of either maintenance or restoration, and assess whether important habitats can be expanded or connected by additional habitat creation
- Record the presence and condition of any important species or features (eg farm ponds or veteran trees) worth specific conservation management
- Assess whether the full requirements of important species can be provided by:
  - maintenance of existing habitats and management
  - restoration of degraded habitats and features through changes in current management
  - creation of new habitat features – check that conditions are right for creation (eg location, soil type, skills and resources)

Step 3 Develop practical actions

- Research the specific management needs of the important habitats and species present and plan the management accordingly – try to integrate the management needs of all important species groups present or likely to be present
- Assess the practicalities of proposed management, for example:
  - Does it fit into the farming system?
  - Is it a cost-effective use of the land identified?
  - Will labour be available at the right time?
- Check availability of resources, such as local provenance seed, or local contractors who can lay hedges

Step 4 Explain the plan to all staff who may be involved in its implementation – this could include:

- the farm manager who oversees operations
- the farm staff who do the cultivations and spraying
- the farmer who rents the grazing land
- the vet who treats the stock
- the contractor who trims the hedges
- the agronomist who advises on pesticide use
- the farm's customers and visitors who might be indirectly paying for it

PART 2
FARMLAND WILDLIFE

2 Small mammals

2.1 Introduction

All of Britain's small mammals (mice, dormice, voles and shrews) make use of farmland to a greater or lesser extent, although their habitat requirements differ. Some species, such as the common and pygmy shrews feed entirely on invertebrates, particularly earthworms, voles are variously herbivorous, while wood mice (Plate 2.1) and harvest mice live on a mixed diet of plant material and insects. Small mammals play an important role in agricultural ecosystems being midway in the food chain; themselves being preyed upon by, for example, birds such as barn owls and larger mammals such as weasels.

As well as an adequate supply of food, all species require suitable habitat for nesting, cover from predators and refuge from farming operations. Despite their varying requirements (Table 2.1), small mammals that live on farmland face a number of common challenges that have

Michael J. Amphlett

Plate 2.1 The wood mouse is one of the most abundant small mammals on farmland and found in arable, grassland and woodland habitats.

Table 2.1 Summary of diet and habitat requirements of small mammal species of farmland.

Species	Diet	Habitat
Common shrew[2]	Mostly invertebrates	Thick grass, bushy scrub, habitats with good vegetative cover
Pygmy shrew[1]	Invertebrates, especially earthworms	Thick grass, bushy scrub, habitats with good vegetative cover
Water shrew[2]	Invertebrates in water and grassland	Thick grass, bushy scrub, habitats with good vegetative cover, especially by water
Bank vole[4]	Fruits, seeds, roots and bark	Hedgerows, field margins
Field vole[2]	Grasses and herbaceous plants	Rough ungrazed grassland
Wood mouse[1]	Mostly seeds and invertebrates, also seedlings, buds, fruit	Arable fields, field margins, grassland, hedgerows, woodland
Yellow-necked mouse[3]	Seedlings, buds, fruit, occasional invertebrates	Woodland and mature hedgerows
House mouse[1]	Mostly grain, seeds and invertebrates	Associated with farm outbuildings especially grain stores and livestock sheds
Harvest mouse[2]	Cereal grains, seeds, fruits, berries, insects	Arable fields, field margins and hedgerows, rough grassland and meadows, ditches
Dormouse[3]	Flowers, pollen, fruits, nuts and berries, aphids	Woodland and mature hedgerows

[1] Occurs in Britain and Ireland; [2] Absent from Ireland; [3] Absent from Scotland and Ireland; [4] Absent from Ireland except where introduced to south-west.

generally become greater with the intensification of farming over the last half century. Habitat destruction and reduction in habitat diversity, increased use of pesticides and fertilisers, and greater mechanisation all impact on the ability of small mammals to survive and reproduce on farmland. In general, the most successful species will be those that are adaptable enough to exploit the unstable, mosaic environment of modern agricultural habitats. Species with specialised requirements are more likely to suffer and require conservation effort.

2.2 Populations and distributions

Surprisingly little is known about long-term trends in abundance of small mammals on farmland. It seems likely that changes in agricultural practice will have affected populations of mice, voles and shrews but, for most species, lack of systematic monitoring means that firm conclusions cannot easily be drawn. One exception to this is the hazel dormouse which has declined severely and is now a designated BAP species. Although largely dependent on ancient deciduous woodland and coppice, the dormouse can be found in hedgerows where there is dense cover and is likely to have been affected in part by the loss and poor management of farmland hedges, and the fragmentation of its woodland habitat.

Of the species which are heavily reliant on farmland, anecdotal information suggests that the harvest mouse in particular may be suffering population declines. In the mid-1990s, a Mammal Society survey found that harvest mice were no longer present at 30% of 800 sites where they had been recorded in the 1970s. Common and pygmy shrews, bank voles, field voles and the ubiquitous wood mouse are all commonly found on farmland, but the extent to which there have been any long-term changes in their population sizes is unknown. All three shrew species, for example, are likely to have been affected by habitat loss and insecticide use reducing their invertebrate prey, but scant information is available. Around farmsteads and outbuildings, the house mouse too has probably become scarcer in recent years, through improved tidiness and bio-security measures, but there are no figures on this.

2.3 Management advice

Factors that are likely to affect small mammals on farmland include habitat destruction and fragmentation, reduction in habitat diversity, pesticide use (which has both direct effects and indirect effects on their plant and invertebrate food resources) and mechanisation.

Modifying management of fields, hedgerows, margins and farm woodlands to counteract some of these impacts can have significant benefits for small mammals. In general, management which increases plant and invertebrate food resources, creates opportunities for nest sites and cover from predators, and creates linkages between habitats for colonisation and dispersal, will help to conserve small mammal populations on farmland. Different species use habitats to different extents (Figure 2.1) and this may also vary throughout the year (Figure 2.2) so increasing the overall diversity of habitats available within a farm will be beneficial to small mammals.

Hedgerows

Hedgerows are very important habitats in the agricultural landscape. They support a rich community of small mammals, including rarer species such as dormice and yellow-necked mice, and more common species such as bank voles and common shrews. Even the adaptable wood mouse, the only small mammal that can live in arable crops year round, makes good use of hedgerows. There are few estimates of the impact of hedgerow removal on small mammals, but it seems likely that problems of hedgerow loss have been exacerbated by changes in their management. For example, since the late 1970s there has been a 65% reduction in the number of hedgerow sites occupied by dormice (Bright and MacPherson 2002) and this decline is primarily due to overly intensive hedgerow management. Current recommendations for dormouse conservation are that most hedgerows are cut at three-yearly intervals, with some left to grow for at least seven to 10 years. It is important that only a minority of hedgerows on a farm are cut in any one year. Coppicing, or laying should be used to restore hedgerows that become gappy, and species-rich hedgerows are especially valuable.

The timing and severity of hedgerow cutting is likely to have a major influence on its suitability for many hedgerow species. For example, mechanically flailing hedgerows has a negative impact on berry production, reducing food availability for species such as dormice. Bank vole populations have also been shown to be reduced by hedgerow flailing. If it is unavoidable, then flailing different aspects of a single hedgerow in rotation may reduce the impact. Other features such as hedgerow height and continuity, species diversity, abundance of seed-producing standards and the nature of the vegetation at the base of the hedge are all important. Recent work has shown that hedges with more trees support more wood mice and that thicker hedgerows have higher numbers of small mammals. A high level of connectivity to adjoining hedgerows typically maintains a higher density of wood mice and bank voles.

As well as being important habitats in themselves, linear features such as hedgerows are widely believed to promote animal dispersal and are commonly referred to as 'corridors'. For dormice, which have suffered from fragmentation and isolation of their populations, suitably managed hedgerows may be crucial to dispersal. This is another important reason to maintain hedgerows in the farmed landscape and, if new hedgerows can be planted to link other types of habitat such as woodlands, this may increase their benefits.

Field margins, beetle banks and ditches

Grassy field margins are important refuges for many species including bank and field voles, harvest mice and pygmy shrews. They are often sown with tussocky species such as cock's-foot that not only enhance populations of invertebrate food, but also provide cover and nesting sites for species such as the bank vole and harvest mouse. Harvest mice, for example, favour cock's-foot, hawthorn and blackthorn as nesting sites on infrequently cut field margins and beetle banks (raised tussocky grass strips across fields). Shore *et al.* (2005) compared small mammal abundance on grassy field margins of different widths with that of conventionally managed field edges with no grassy margin. They found that bank vole (Plate 2.2) and common shrew abundances were higher on the grassy field margins in autumn, and that wider

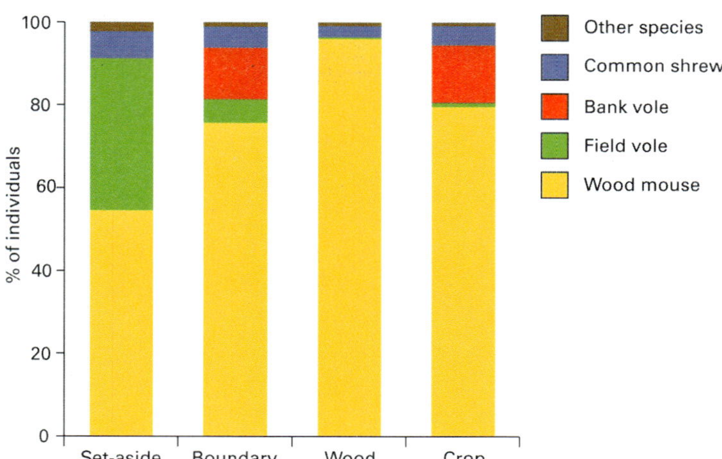

Figure 2.1
Percentage of each species in small mammal communities live-trapped in set-aside, field boundaries (hedgerow, field margin and crop edge), crop and woodlots (<1 ha). 'Other' species were house mouse, yellow-necked mouse, harvest mouse and pygmy shrew. From Tattershall and Macdonald (2003).

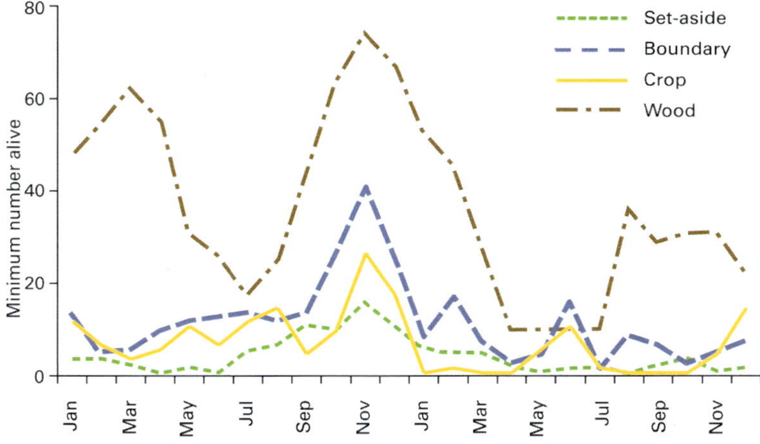

Figure 2.2
Habitat use by wood mice varies seasonally, and with farming operations (especially harvest); increasing habitat diversity will benefit small mammals. From Macdonald *et al.* (2000).

Michael J. Amphlett

Plate 2.2 Woodlands, hedgerows and grassy field margins are important habitats for the bank vole.

margins and those adjacent to a hedgerow had greatest numbers of bank voles.

Grassy margins act as buffers, helping to protect the hedgerow and hedge base vegetation from farming operations and spray drift. They are particularly valuable if they have a diversity of structure, which can be encouraged by not cutting every year. Reducing the frequency of cutting, and not cutting field margins during the spring and summer when small mammals are nesting, as well as reducing other disturbance such as driving along margins, will have positive impacts on small mammal populations.

Some studies have shown that the presence of ditches can encourage bank voles and yellow-necked mice. Ditches provide ample burrowing habitat for small mammals, and the vegetation associated with them will increase plant and invertebrate food resources, and give cover from predators. Tall ditch vegetation, such as reeds, makes especially good nesting sites for harvest mice.

In-field areas: crops and grassland

Cropped areas provide plant and invertebrate food for small mammals and, at some times during the year, cover from predators and nest sites. In other ways, though, they are an unforgiving habitat for small mammals, which must contend not only with agrochemical applications, but also the removal of cover at harvest, quickly followed by ploughing, leaving bare ground over winter. The physical process of harvesting has little direct effect on wood mice in fields while they remain in their burrows but the removal of cover greatly increases exposure of attack by predators. Radio-tracking studies have shown how wood mouse numbers decline following harvest due to the combined effects of predation and emigration from fields. Nonetheless, there are ways to help small mammals survive in this challenging environment.

Perhaps the most important of these is, where possible, to reduce the use of herbicides and insecticides within the crop. Conservation headlands (Plate 2.3) where the outer 6 m or so of cereal fields receive reduced selective pesticide applications, can be beneficial. They are widely supported through agri-environment scheme funding. Conservation headlands have higher abundances of insects and arable weeds, both of which are eaten by small mammals such as harvest mice and wood mice – the latter have been shown to forage preferentially in patches of weeds, particularly black-grass, sterile brome and wild oats. In radio-tracking studies, wood mice spent their time, in order of preference, in unsprayed headlands, selectively sprayed headlands, followed by sprayed headlands and, least of all in mid-field areas. Organic farming may have benefits for small mammals by increasing the abundance of plant and insect food resources throughout the entire cropped area, with knock-on benefits for the mammal species that feed on them.

Less is known about the effects of grassland management on small mammals. It seems likely that more intensive management for silage production, and increased stocking densities, will have had negative impacts on small mammals. Field voles, for example, rely on rough, ungrazed grassland. Although they are thought to be Britain's most numerous small mammal, this is on the basis of poor data and may be an out-dated view –

P Thompson (The Game Conservancy)

Plate 2.3 Conservation headlands can increase food resources for small mammals such as wood mice.

contemporary information on their true status is lacking. The field vole is well known for its fluctuations in population size which tend to occur in 3–5 year cycles, but the reasons behind these fluctuations are not fully understood. Field voles are the main food of British barn owls (except in Ireland, where voles are absent), forming up to 90% of their diet – in years when vole numbers are low fewer young barn owls may be reared. However, the principles of management for grassland are broadly the same as that for arable and field margin habitats: increasing sward diversity to enhance plant and invertebrate food resources, reducing pesticide and fertiliser inputs where possible, and minimising disturbance to the sward will all help improve the habitat for field vole and other small mammal populations.

As well as having widespread indirect effects on small mammals through reducing plant and invertebrate food availability and altering habitat structure, pesticides can also have directly toxic effects. Of the pesticides currently in use, molluscicides and rodenticides probably pose the greatest threat to small mammals. Wood mice, for example, are particularly at risk from molluscicides since they are the commonest small mammal species in arable fields and are known to consume methiocarb pellets. However, the impact on their populations will depend on several factors such as the availability of alternative food sources and the method of application.

Rodenticides pose an obvious risk to non-target mammal species. Consumption of bait is the direct route of exposure for small mammals – other predators and scavengers are exposed to rodenticides by consuming contaminated prey. Use of rodenticides around, rather than within, farm buildings, and particularly in fields and woods, will present greater risks to non-target wildlife than restricting their use to inside buildings, although house mice and wood mice will remain vulnerable.

Set-aside

A range of management options is available, including how set-aside is established and how often it is relocated, but the land must have a green cover over winter, and this must be destroyed annually with herbicides or by cutting. Set-aside can also be configured either as field margins or as larger blocks.

These different management options all have the potential to impact on small mammals found on set-aside, including common species such as wood mice, field voles and common and pygmy shrews. For example, after harvest, when fields are bare, studies have shown, first, that wood mice prefer uncut rather than cut areas of set-aside and, second, that set-aside configured as margins next to hedgerow may have more abundant and diverse small mammal communities than larger blocks of set-aside. In these studies, wood mice were more numerous in margins, and bank voles, a hedgerow species, did not venture into the centre of set-aside fields. Long-term set-aside is particularly valuable – as set-aside ages there are changes in species composition, with field voles progressively becoming a greater component of the community, and diversity of small mammals also increasing over time.

Woodland

Many of our native mammals are woodland species, reflecting the prehistoric dominance of this habitat. Most small mammals either require, or benefit from, the cover provided by woodland or scrub, but little is known about the actual amounts of woodland they require, or the effects of woodland shape and arrangement in the landscape. Creating or retaining woodland within the farmed landscape will greatly encourage a rich community of small mammals and help to buffer populations against the effects of farm operations.

Broadleaf woodland is used, at least in part, by most small mammal species. However, the ways in which it is managed can change its value, particularly for species with very specialised requirements like the dormouse, which is dependent on ancient semi-natural woodlands. The dormouse's ability to digest woody material is limited, and it needs to feed on flowers, fruit and insects to survive. Dormice need a very diverse woodland habitat with trees and shrubs that fruit in different seasons, to ensure a continuous food supply over the growing season. Woods that are managed to reduce the canopy cover and maintain the understorey, for example by coppicing, are particularly suitable for this species. Where woodlands can be linked across farmland by mature, continuous hedgerow there will be even greater benefits for more sedentary species such as dormice.

Summary

Habitat	Management	Will especially benefit
Hedgerows	Wider hedgerows with some trees especially beneficial. Cut infrequently. Time cutting operations to allow fruit/berry production. Create hedgerows to connect to each other and link other habitats such as woodland in the landscape.	All small mammal species
Arable field margins and beetle banks	Create grassy field margin swards and cut infrequently. More species-rich seed mixtures will enhance plant, seed and invertebrate food supplies. Margins situated next to hedgerows and ditches especially valuable.	Bank vole, field vole harvest mouse, wood mouse, common and pygmy shrews
Ditches	Maintain ditches – manage banks on rotation similar to field margins and maintain water levels where possible.	Water shrew, yellow-necked mouse
Crops and grassland	Reduce fertiliser, herbicide, insecticide and molluscicide inputs. Create conservation headlands. Reduce stocking densities in grassland.	Wood mouse, harvest mouse, common and pygmy shrews; field vole (grassland)
Set-aside	Long-term set-aside especially valuable. Use a species rich mixture if establishing long-term set-aside. Leave uncut where possible.	Wood mouse, field vole, common and pygmy shrews
Woodland	Maintain woodlots in the farmed landscape. Diversity of native tree and shrub species especially beneficial. Manage by coppicing.	Dormouse, yellow-necked mouse, wood mouse bank vole

Further reading

Battersby J (ed.) (2005) *UK Mammals: species status and population trends*. JNCC/ Tracking Mammals Partnership 2005.

Bright P and MacPherson D (2002) Hedgerow management, dormice and biodiversity. *English Nature Report No 454*. English Nature, Peterborough.

Macdonald D W and Tattersall F H (2001) *Britain's mammals: the challenge for conservation*. People's Trust for Endangered Species.

Macdonald D W, Feber R E, Johnson P J and Tattersall F (2000) Ecological experiments in farmland conservation. In: *The ecological consequences of environmental heterogeneity* (eds M J Hutchings, E A John and A J A Stewart), pp 357–378. British Ecological Society Symposium. Blackwell Scientific Publications, Oxford.

Shore R F, Meek W R, Sparks T H, Pywell R F and Nowakowski M (2005) Will Environmental Stewardship enhance small mammal abundance on intensively managed farmland? *Mammal Review*, 35, 277–284.

Tattersall F H and Macdonald D W (2003) Wood mice in the arable ecosystem. In: *Conservation and conflict: mammals and farming in Britain* (eds F H Tattersall and W J Manley), pp 82–96. Linnean Society Occasional Publications, Westbury Publishing.

Tattersall F H and Manley W J (eds) (2003) *Conservation and conflict: mammals and farming in Britain*. Linnean Society Occasional Publications, Westbury Publishing.

3 Brown hare and Irish hare

3.1 Introduction

Brown hares are open country animals that were originally adapted to the grassland steppe that occurs north and east of the Black Sea. Closely related species, with similar ecology, are found on the African savannah and American prairie. With the spread of European farming from the Levant across to the Atlantic seaboard and the woodland clearance that accompanied it, a new steppe-like landscape was created. This suited the brown hare better than it did the other north European hare, the mountain hare, which is better adapted to uplands, scrub and woodland fringes. Brown hares were probably brought to Britain in late Iron Age or during Roman times, when our countryside was dominated by mixed farming.

The Irish hare is a native sub-species of mountain hare that is found throughout the uplands and lowlands of Ireland. Irish hares are the only native lagomorph in Ireland, though brown hares have been introduced for sporting purposes and are common in some localised areas. Numbers of Irish hares are believed to have declined markedly through the 20th century. The habitat requirements of the Irish hare are broadly similar to those of the brown hare and there is a general understanding of factors that may have caused a decline in numbers. Habitat management could enable a population recovery, if it is well targeted.

3.2 Declines in the 20th century

It is not clear how common hares were under medieval farming systems, but it is likely that their numbers were boosted by 17th century land enclosures and the new crop rotations that followed. No doubt, the rise in 19th century gamekeeping for gamebirds also helped hares of both species because their main predator, the fox, was relentlessly controlled. By 1880, hares were probably at their peak of abundance across Britain. This, as well as the burgeoning rabbit population, led directly to the Ground Game Act (1880) which gives tenant farmers the right to control rabbits and hares – indicating that for many farmers, brown hares were a bit of pest – indeed in some areas of England they still are and the Ground Game Act has not been repealed.

The game books kept by rural estates during the 20th century illustrate the changing fortunes of hares, indeed the details of numbers shot each year provide the only source of long-term data on hare numbers until very recent years.

For brown hares these records show a decline in numbers between the wars, probably associated with a decline in arable farming, a further peak in abundance in the late 1950s to the early 1960s (probably as a consequence of *Myxomatosis* killing most of the rabbits) and a progressive decline between about 1962 and 1990. Nationally this looks like a drop of around 75%.

For Irish hares, game bags show a marked decline since around 1914, related to changes in Irish land management, to the point where organised hare shooting more or less disappeared. Factors such as break-up of keepered estates, loss of cover and refuge areas (rushes, scrub and hedgerows), agricultural improvement of grasslands and increased disturbance from farm machinery are all believed to have had a role.

The decline of hares is not unique to Britain and Ireland but has occurred throughout Western Europe, more or less wherever hare bag numbers have been recorded. Both hare species have been designated as Biodiversity Action Plan species because of their declines, and not because hares are in any sense nationally rare.

3.3 Hare ecology

The British plan for brown hares aims to double their numbers by 2010. The All-Ireland Species Action Plan for Irish hares

David Kjaer

Mike Brown Photography

Plate 3.1 (left)
Brown hare

Plate 3.2 (right)
Irish hare

aims to demonstrate a population increase by 2010, maintain the range of the species and increase the area and quality of suitable habitat.

While poaching and disease can and do have local impacts on hare numbers the mains reasons for the overall reduction in number seem to be modern farming systems and predation by increased numbers of foxes, with the former probably exacerbating the latter. To improve hare abundance we need to apply our understanding of hare ecology.

Two things that are not generally appreciated about hares are that they are nocturnal and that they are quite social. Just because you see hares on their own during the day does not mean that is when they prefer to be out and about. Go out at night in winter with a spotlight and binoculars and you will find them feeding on winter corn, grass or oilseed rape. Chances are they will not be alone but there will be others nearby, feeding in the same field.

Diet

A hare's digestive habits are tied to this pattern of activity. It grazes at night, filling its stomach with fresh young greens, and then rests during the day while digesting what it has eaten and at the same time consuming the soft faecal pellets it passes during the day. It eats these directly as they are passed out of its anus (a process known as refection).

Hares are selective grazers and browsers that are partial to most farm crops when they are short and digestible, but they also like wild plants including annual weeds, perennials and shrubs. They also have a penchant for eating the bark off newly planted trees and hedgerow shrubs. To get forage year round, hares have to move around the farm, switching from crop to crop as each becomes palatable.

For brown hares, radio-tracking on mixed farmland has revealed that a typical sequence might be: winter wheat in mid- to late winter, then any spring crops until late April, after that, in summer, the grass leys, pastures (without the livestock) set-aside and field margins. In autumn, break crops such as stubble turnips provide good forage, as do stubbles which are greening up with weeds and volunteers. In late autumn and early winter, oilseed rape is probably the favourite crop. Although brown hares tend to shift their grazing around the farm in response to crop development and grazing livestock, hares

David Kjaer

Plate 3.3 Brown hares benefit from a wide mix of crops to provide them with food and cover at different times throughout the year.

do not necessarily rest where they feed. If it is a big field of winter wheat, after a nights grazing they may simply dig a scrape in the middle and settle down for the day. At other times, they may commute, resting on one field and feeding in another. This applies particularly in summer when their foraging may be confined to small field margins and tracksides. On mixed farmland, brown hares forage over a range of about 50 hectares, normally taking in about eight different fields.

Irish hares are more typically found on grasslands and moorlands, especially unimproved, species-rich grasslands. They feed on a variety of grasses, but may also eat sedges, shrubs and tree shoots. Like brown hares they use a variety of habitats moving between sources of food and cover as they become available during the year.

Breeding

The breeding ecology of brown and Irish hares is similar. Given the right conditions hares are prolific breeders and indeed, it is possible in some productive environments to come across leverets in almost any month of the year. However, normal breeding starts in February and ends in September with a peak in births in May and June. The typical litter size is 2–3 young and a female may have around three litters a year; bigger litters are not uncommon in the case of the brown hare. Mild springs and prolonged summers can extend the season and cold wet summers tend to reduce leveret survival, so there can be a big variation in autumn numbers depending on summer weather. A female hare will drop her young in a quiet corner of her home range and return each night (one hour after sunset) to suckle them briefly for about five minutes in every 24 hours. The young leverets gradually separate themselves, but they return to their original birth site to be suckled each night.

3.4 Management advice

Food and cover are watchwords for both brown and Irish hares on farmland.

Management advice for brown hare

Both food and cover need to be provided in the context of an open landscape, not hemmed in by woodland or large hedgerows around small fields. Some kinds of country, for example heavily wooded parts of the Weald, simply may not suit hares and there may not be much point in trying to bring them back. Also, countryside heavily intersected by roads or on an urban fringe may not be able to sustain a hare population – although there are some good examples where it can. In other places, the landscape may be fine but the forage and cover combination may be missing. This is where some habitat conservation can be usefully applied. Broadly speaking this can be broken down to two strategies – improving cover on livestock farms, or improving summer food supply on arable farms. On mixed farms, with both arable and livestock, habitat conditions are normally good.

Livestock farms

Hares generally do not like high densities of livestock and will avoid fields with moderate to high stock levels. However, when a pasture is given a rest and livestock temporarily move out, the hares gradually come back – only to move out again when the stock is put back. While there is usually some grazing for hares on a livestock farm very often there is little or no cover. For adult hares this is probably not much of problem – they can sit out in the open in most weathers and they can out-run most predators (except perhaps poachers' dogs). Young leverets are, however, very vulnerable to foxes especially at night – and probably to some raptors as well. Predation of leverets may be the cause of the absence or very low numbers of hares in some areas.

Recommended measures under agri-environment schemes:

- *Rough grass field margins and corners in grass fields.* Ideal for providing small pockets of cover around the farm and likely to help reduce leveret losses to grass mowing.
- *Wild bird cover crops.* Good for birds, but hares love them too. It provides both cover and some food. Kale and cereals will suit hares very well.
- *Low-input grassland management.* Hares certainly like wild herbs and grasses so these pastures and meadows will be an asset to the hare population.

Arable farms

Arable farmland is the best countryside for brown hares. Old-fashioned farming with grass leys, and spring and winter cereals in a patchwork landscape is perfect for hares. This gives them food and cover across the farm in all seasons. However, modern rotations with winter cereals and oilseed rape provide grazing in winter, but very little in summer when crops are ripening. In summer, hares may be reduced to nibbling around the field margins and tracksides.

Set-aside has probably done more than anything else to improve hare numbers over the last decade. Although not designed with conservation in mind it has broken up the big continuous blocks of cereal and oilseed rape. To make the most of set-aside for hares or any other species, deploy it round the farm in small areas and, if possible, plant it up with wild bird crops.

Recommended measures under agri-environment schemes:

- *Six-metre wide buffer strips.* Ideal if you mow half of the width of the strip annually to give some short summer grazing along the field boundary, as well as additional long grass cover in winter.
- *Six-metre uncropped cultivated margins.* An ideal option if it works. On the right kind of land, a variety of annual flowers and grasses provide a perfect mixed salad for hares in summer.
- *Conservation headlands with no fertiliser.* A good option for gamebirds, for which it was designed, but good for hares too as it provides a thin crop with a variety of food plants.
- *Over-wintered stubbles.* Very good for hares primarily because it is a whole-field option. The stubble itself is a good hiding place and the volunteers and weeds add variety to the winter diet. However, the most useful aspect is likely to be that this option is followed by a spring crop which will give food into the early summer.

Predation

For some species, like the brown hare, habitat management may only be half a solution. If enhancing hare populations is a priority, one needs to make sure the hare population is not being subject to severe poaching or to heavy predation. Fox control may not be appropriate everywhere, and it certainly is expensive in manpower, but it can have a dramatic effect on hare numbers. At The Game Conservancy Trust's 333 ha Allerton farm at Loddington in Leicestershire, between 1992 and 2001, the hare population increased from a population of around 30 to some 300 within four years, as result of habitat improvement and fox control, but has shown a decline since the cessation of fox control in 2002.

Management advice for Irish hare

In terms of habitat enhancement, maintenance and restoration of a patchwork of species-rich grassland for food and rushes and scrub for cover is most likely to aid the recovery of the Irish hare in lowland and marginal environments. As the grass in sileage fields grows, hares tend to stay in these fields because they provide both food and cover, and this can make them and their young vulnerable to rolling and mowing. So, it is possible that modification of sileage production plans could improve hare breeding success. Hares also are affected to a lesser extent by disturbance where there is a moderate to high stocking rate, so extensive grazing may be beneficial.

Arable options, particularly spring cropping, wild bird covers and grass buffer strips to increase the variety of food plants and cover, may also benefit Irish hares, but the limited area of arable farmland in Ireland means that these are less important measures for this species than the brown hare.

Further reading

Environment and Heritage Service (2005) Irish hare. Wildlife factsheet 005. www.ehsni.gov.uk/education/factsheets.shtml

Reynolds J C and Tapper S C (1995) Predation by foxes *Vulpes vulpes* on brown hares *Lepus europaeus* in central southern England, and its potential impact on annual population growth. *Wildlife Biology* 1, 145–58.

Smith R K, Jennings N V and Harris S (2005) A quantitative analysis of the abundance and demography of European hares *Lepus europaeus* in relation to habitat type, intensity of agriculture and climate. *Mammal Review* 35, 1–24.

Tapper S C and Barnes R F W (1986) Influence of farming practice on the ecology of the brown hare (*Lepus europaeus*). *Journal of Applied Ecology* 23, 39–52.

4 Bats

4.1 Introduction

Farmland represents one of the most important landscape types for British bats. It can provide all of their key requirements – insect-rich feeding habitats, roosting sites in farm buildings and in trees, and flyways, such as hedgerows, connecting the two. All British bat species occur in the agricultural landscape to some extent. Most bat activity is associated with the non-crop component of agricultural landscapes – trees and woodland, water and riparian habitats, hedges and traditional farm buildings, but grassland, in particular pasture grazed by livestock (especially cattle), is also of importance. The ranges over which bats can fly in a night means that they may venture beyond the boundaries of one farm onto another or into neighbouring land-use types. Additionally bats may come onto a farm to feed from some distance away, for example from a roost in a suburban building. A whole-landscape approach to management is required, and conservation activities will be most beneficial if implemented on a whole-farm scale and if neighbouring landowners are encouraged to take up options too. As an example, greater horseshoe bats have typically been shown to forage over a distance of 4–5 km from their summer roosts and 1–2 km from their winter hibernation sites. Farmers entering upper tiers of agri-environment schemes within a 4–5 km radius of known maternity roosts and hibernacula of greater horseshoe bats have been encouraged to take up options for their benefit.

4.2 Populations and distributions

Populations of many bat species are believed to have declined substantially in the last century, both in Britain and Ireland, and across Europe. Changes in farming practices have been a major driver of these declines. The species that may be in the locality of a farm can be inferred from range maps and from the proximity of bat records held, for example, by local records centres and local bat groups. Bats are nocturnal creatures and are often seldom noticed, except perhaps around the farmyard at dusk on a warm summer's evening or if a roost is known in one of the farm buildings. Surveys with bat detectors

Hugh Clark/Bat Conservation Trust

Plate 4.1
Pipistrelle

are the quickest and easiest way to get a preliminary view of the abundance and diversity of species on farmland. These are best done on calm, warm, rain-free evenings between May and September. A local bat group may be able to help and also to give information about bats.

Causes of decline

Bats have complex requirements that vary seasonally and differ according to species, sex and age. Reduction or loss of any one component of their requirements can detrimentally affect their conservation status, but usually several factors will go hand in hand resulting in a negative impact on a population. A combination of factors have been linked to declines, either operating on bats themselves (eg loss of roosts and loss of connecting features such as hedgerows or tree-lines), or on their insect prey.

Loss of roosting places, particularly those used by maternity colonies of breeding females, can be devastating. In the farmed landscape, the greatest impact on bat roosts is likely to have been the trend for conversion of traditional farm buildings, particularly barns, into dwellings or other uses, thereby making them unsuitable for

Table 4.1 Factors associated with changes in farming that have contributed to the decline of insects preyed on by bats.

Factor	Description
Landscape and cropping pattern	Removal of boundary features such as hedgerows and non-crop habitats to create larger field sizes in larger farm holdings, particularly of arable and improved grassland, results in the loss of species associated with such habitats. Cropping pattern influences insect abundance, for example different crops vary widely in their beetle assemblages. Diptera such as craneflies are influenced by management that affects vegetation height and density, for example where oilseed rape precedes a winter wheat crop, emerging adult craneflies may fail to disperse from under the canopy.
Farming system	Organic farming prohibits the use of synthetic pesticides and is generally less intensive than conventional farming. For example it tends to use more traditional techniques including crop rotations, crop diversification, green manures/composts and encouragement of natural pest control populations. These practices are likely to have fewer negative consequences for invertebrates, however some organic farms can still be fairly intensive, for example by removal of hedgerows or by mechanical weed control
Agrochemical usage	The wide use of synthetic pesticides (herbicides, insecticides and fungicides) in conventional farming is likely to have had the greatest impact on invertebrates through direct toxicity, but also indirectly by restricting insect food supply or altering their habitat. Effects are species specific and vary according to the mode and frequency of application.
Avermectins	Avermectins are a group of chemicals used in modern livestock endo-parasite control practices. They have been found to be harmful to non-target dung invertebrates, in particular dung flies, and dung beetles whose larvae are killed by pesticide residues in animal dung.
Fertiliser practice	Fertiliser impacts on insects vary according to the type and frequency of application. Bat foraging activity decreases if waters are polluted.
Cutting and grazing	Grassland management that alters the structure and composition of vegetation can have major impacts on invertebrate abundance and species composition. Short homogeneous sward structures often hold fewer invertebrates.
Drainage	The widespread installation of under-field drainage in the 1970s and 1980s accompanied substantial modification of river catchments in southern Britain, and had a devastating impact on insects, particularly on the Diptera (true flies). The shift from 3–4 year rotational ditch clearance by hand to regular large-scale mechanical clearance has also resulted in large networks of ditches unsuitable for many species that require bankside sediments and vegetation.
Soil cultivation	Ploughing tends to reduce populations of fly and beetle larvae in soils and can also be detrimental to spiders, moths and bugs.
Hedgerow removal	Insects use hedgerows as courtship and breeding sites, feeding sites, as refuges from predators, hibernation sites or as shelter. Removal of hedgerows consequently results in reduced insect species diversity. Fragmentation of the landscape through hedgerow removal also leaves fewer connecting features for bats to use in moving between feeding areas and roosts.

bats to inhabit. Roosts in trees (for example mature hedgerow trees, in-field trees and small farm woodlands) may be lost when trees are felled or areas of woodland are cleared.

Changes in farming practices are considered to have resulted in a reduction in the overall abundance and diversity of insect prey. This is likely to have played a major part in reducing bat numbers. The main factors that have the potential to impact insect populations are outlined in Table 4.1.

4.3 Habitat requirements

The three basic habitat requirements for bats on farmland are places to roost, foraging areas rich in their insect prey, and commuting routes to facilitate their travel between roosts and feeding areas both within farmland and to and from the landscape beyond.

Bats roost in a variety of locations depending on the species, sex and time of year. For some species, mature trees are important, whereas others make use of built structures such as barns and farmhouses or bridges and culverts. Roosts may not necessarily be on the farm, but the bats may come onto farmland to feed and vice versa.

During spring, breeding females gather to form maternity colonies where they give birth and raise their single offspring. Young are born around the end of June and beginning of July and reach independence around the end of August. Colonies are particularly susceptible to disturbance of their roosts between these times. Rich feeding areas close to maternity roosts in the late spring and summer months are especially important for meeting the high-energy requirements of pregnant and lactating females and to provide food nearby for young on their early foraging flights.

Every night bats leave their roosts and fly to feeding sites where they use echolocation to catch their insect prey. The method of prey capture varies between species; for example some catch insects on the wing (known as either fast or slow 'hawking'), others 'trawl' insects from the surface of water bodies, several 'glean' insects from vegetation or the ground, and a few hunt from perches (also known as 'fly-catching').

J J Kaczanow/Bat Conservation Trust

Plate 4.2 Greater horseshoe bat

The composition of bats' diets is influenced by their mode of feeding. Nine of the 17 British bat species eat mainly true flies (Diptera), all species eat moths and butterflies (Lepidoptera) to some extent, and many eat beetles (Coleoptera). True bugs, plant hoppers and leaf hoppers (Hemiptera) and spiders (Arachnida) are taken to a lesser extent.

Larger bats, such as the greater horsehoe and serotine feed on cockchafers (maybugs), dung beetles and moths. Bats have been known to land on the ground in pasture to catch adult insects emerging from pupation in the soil. Cockchafers and dung beetles are particularly associated with permanent cattle-grazed pasture, as are numerous species of dung flies that are taken by smaller bat species.

There is often particularly rich feeding to be had over water and this is exploited by several bat species, most notably the

Welsh Assembly Government

Plate 4.3 Cattle grazed pasture provides plenty of dung flies and beetles for bats to feed on.

Daubenton's bat and the soprano pipistrelle, both of which feed on emerging aquatic insects such as midges, gnats and caddis flies. Traditionally managed hay meadows and wet meadows generally have diverse plant communities supporting a wide variety of insects. Barbastelle bats in particular seem to favour wetter meadows where they feed on micromoths.

The common pipistrelle is a generalist that utilises many different habitats for feeding. It is the species most likely to be found feeding almost anywhere on the farm including the farmhouse garden. Lesser horseshoe, brown long-eared and Natterer's bats snatch insects directly from foliage and consequently seldom venture from the cover of woodland or thick hedgerows.

Bats use linear features such as hedgerows, woodland edges and sheltered ditches to navigate and give protection from wind while flying. These features also tend to be richer in prey than the habitats they border. Although arable fields are among the agricultural habitats least used by bats, their value can be enhanced by good field edge management, for example by encouraging species-rich hedges and maintaining chemical-free buffer strips.

In winter, bats may feed during milder weather. At this time, good quality feeding habitat close to hibernacula may be essential to their survival. Disused mines, caves, old railway tunnels and bunkers, etc may be used by bats for hibernation if they provide stable low temperatures and high humidity with little human disturbance. Features such as old military fortifications (pill boxes) and tunnels can be enhanced for use by hibernating bats.

4.4 Management advice

The objectives of management to conserve bats on agricultural land should be to protect, provide and enhance roosting opportunities and to create a network of well-connected insect-rich habitats around the farm. Good management of species-rich hedgerows, waterways, woodland, and field margins will benefit most species of bat by increasing the abundance and spatial distribution of insect groups on which they feed. Maintenance, restoration or recreation of semi-improved grassland is essential for some species. Low-input crop management is also important for providing insects more generally across the farmed landscape.

Effort should be made to tailor options, especially where maternity colonies of species with particular requirements are known to be in the vicinity. For example, greater horseshoe bats and serotines need a good supply of dung insects. Management to boost insect prey should be implemented throughout a radius of at least 5 km around maturnity roosts of such species. However, this distance varies according to species present and habitat quality.

Where hibernation sites are known it is important that these are protected and access is maintained for the bats, but also that the surrounding land is managed to be as insect-rich as possible. Locating food during mild winter weather may mean the difference between a bat making it through the winter and not. Good farmland management to maximise insect production within 1 km or more of underground sites used by hibernating bats is recommended.

Arable land

Bats occasionally feed over arable crops but usually focus on the surrounding edge habitats that provide more insects. A conservation headland in the crop, or a buffer strip around the field, which has no insecticide or herbicide applications will increase the number of insects and buffer the effect of spray drift on field boundary vegetation. Taking field corners out of production for tree planting or allowing grassland and scrub to develop will also increase the variety of habitat available in the arable landscape.

Rough grass field margins, which are cut no more than once every five years, will boost numbers of many insects eaten by bats, but a diversity of margin vegetation, by including wild flowers in the mix, or establishing some pollen and nectar mixtures, will increase the diversity of foraging habitats available. Different field-margin types may provide insects at different times of the year.

Insecticides should only be used where essential, and prophylactic use of insecticides should be avoided. If application thresholds exist, then insecticide should only be applied when pest numbers exceeds the threshold. Broad-spectrum insecticides should be avoided where possible.

Grassland

Low-input grassland supports a number of insects on which bats depend. Try to minimise ploughing and reseeding which kills soil-dwelling insect larvae. Avoid rolling, harrowing or fertilising, or the use of pesticides, particularly where roosts of horseshoe, barbastelle, noctule or serotine bats occur in the locality.

Uncut margins should be left along boundaries and in inaccessible areas to provide habitats for insects. Limiting the use of fertilisers allows a greater range of plant species to survive and therefore benefits the insects that feed on them.

Areas of winter grazing can be beneficial close to hibernacula of species which feed on semi-improved pastures, such as greater horseshoe bats.

Wet areas

Rivers, ponds, boggy areas and ditches are particularly good for flies and moths. Manage, restore or reinstate sheltered farm ponds, marshes, ditches and streams, together with wider wetland areas, but take care not to damage existing areas of high conservation value. Plant or manage trees and shrubs on the windward side of ponds and waterways to provide still, sheltered conditions for insects to congregate in and to help bats to feed and drink more easily on the wing. Good water quality is important. Try to retain a variety of different habitats along watercourses. Reduce the impact of management on insects associated with the bankside and submerged vegetation by cutting small areas at a time and limiting livestock access. Cut or clear sections of the ditch on a rotation, rather than all in the same year.

Welsh Assembly Government

Plate 4.4 Recontructing flyways by replanting hedgerows helps bats move through the landscape.

Hedgerow management

Hedgerows and tree lines often provide links between roosting and feeding sites and can themselves provide foraging areas. Hedges should be continuous, tall and wide; ideally a height of at least 3 m, with a mix of native species including young saplings. Hedgerow trees provide shelter and feeding perches and may also provide way markers allowing bats to get their bearings while commuting.

Restore and create hedgerows to provide a continuous network of sheltered flyways for bats. Thick well-developed hedgerows are favoured and tend to have more insects. A diversity of hedge sizes should be maintained in keeping with the landscape character. Avoid coppicing or laying long stretches of tall hedgerows in one year – it is better to spread the work over as long a period as possible and ensure that a network of tall hedges remains, particularly connecting wooded areas of the farm with ideal foraging habitats.

Trees and woodland

Trees with woodpecker holes or that have been damaged, have rot holes, cracks, splits and loose bark etc are most likely to contain roosts. Dark staining under the roost entrance could be from bat droppings or grease from their fur, but not all roosts have this. Bat roosts are protected by law whether or not bats are present at the time, so you should always check for the presence of bats in holes and crevices before undertaking any tree work. You are advised to have a survey conducted by a bat expert and/or contact the SNCO for advice before proceeding. A Habitats Regulations licence will be needed to carry out work on a tree known to be used by bats where that work would disturb bats or change the roost in any way. Keep standing all old or dying trees, and dead wood, where this can be done safely. In-field and in-hedgerow trees may be as valuable as trees in woodland.

Where possible, fell in sections and leave the wood on the ground for at least 24 hours for any bats that may be present to escape. Preferably leave intact and in situ to benefit deadwood fauna.

Woodland edge with a mix of native deciduous species will support higher numbers of insects, especially when it provides shelter from the wind, which is also beneficial for foraging bats. Mature trees generally support greater numbers and diversity of insect species.

All ancient and semi-natural woodland should be retained. Old orchards can also be good foraging areas for bats, provided insecticide use is restricted. Help to provide continuity in roosting opportunities in broadleaved woodland by maintaining blocks of mature woodland (at least 35 years old), and trees with potential roost cavities, and by limiting the amount that is clear felled at one time.

Conifer plantations should incorporate corridors and edges of native broadleaved trees. Bat boxes can be useful in woodlands lacking hollow trees, but they are not a replacement for a good quality diverse landscape with numerous natural opportunities for roosting.

Plant new blocks of native deciduous woodland, though not on land of high conservation value. Aim to form connections with existing woods. Try to incorporate meandering rides and glades of at least 10–15 m across, which should be managed without insecticides to benefit populations of moths on which bats can feed.

Anti-parasitic drug regimes

Livestock dung hosts many different insects that contribute to its breakdown and that provide food for bats. However, modern livestock endo-parasite control practices, most notably the use of avermectins, can kill dung insects, in particular of dung flies. Even if they do not directly kill the insects they may affect the insects' ability to reproduce.

The method of application and its timing affects the duration of the drugs' persistence in the animal and consequently its presence in the dung and its effect on dung insects. Bolus or repeated injections over the summer are likely to have the greatest impact and should be avoided where possible. Alternative treatments should be considered, particularly when stock are feeding in fields around maternity roosts. Organic cattle grazed pasture has been encouraged close to maternity colonies of greater horseshoe bats. This is particularly beneficial to juvenile bats when first flying and foraging because of the high proportion of dung beetles taken at this age.

Organic management systems

Owing to the lack of agrochemicals and emphasis on crop rotations and features supporting natural predators, the habitats on organically managed farms are often of higher quality and the landscape structure more diverse than conventional farms. General bat activity, and more specifically bat foraging activity, has been found to be higher on organic than conventional farms. Similarly, insect abundance was found to be greater on organic farms and to have more of the key insect families important to bats as food. Organic and less intensive management of farmland may therefore benefit bats by permitting their prey numbers to increase.

The use of organic fertilisers such as farmyard manure and slurry generally benefit dung fauna including flies and beetles important to bats. Cattle manure is preferable to pig manure. Excessive use of slurries can negatively impact some groups due to oxygen depletion and toxicity of chemicals in the slurry so care should be taken.

Traditional farm buildings

Traditional buildings, such as barns and farmhouses, may be used by bats throughout the year. Access points may be in timberwork, under tiles, behind flashing, under eaves or through open windows, doors and other openings. Tiny gaps in the structure of farm buildings (less than 1 cm) will allow pipistrelle bats to enter, eg over doors, under eaves or into the gable apex. At night bats will enter more open buildings for rest periods between feeding bouts or to hang while eating a moth. Other buildings, such as military pillboxes may be adapted to accommodate bats (see Mitchell-Jones and McLeish, 2004).

Few bats are visible when roosting as most tuck themselves deep into crevices. Greater and lesser horseshoe bats tend to hang free from the roof lining or roof beams and may be visible in attics. Brown long-eared bats are sometimes visible along the ridgeline of timber-framed roofs. Natterer's bats prefer to secrete themselves into mortise joints, such as those found in large supporting beams in traditional barns. Often the only indication will be collections of harmless droppings on the floor, or the sight of bats emerging in the evenings. Bats may become active early in the evening and fly inside large indoor spaces, such as barns or extensive attics before emerging. Some may feed inside barns, particularly where animals are housed and insect numbers are therefore high.

All bat roosts are protected by law regardless of whether bats are present or not. If you know a building is used as a roost at any time of year, you must obtain advice from a bat expert and/or the SNCO before starting building or maintenance work to identify whether your proposals will disturb the bats or affect the roost in any way. Examples of work that can disturb bats and/or affect roosts include conversions (eg from a barn to a dwelling), remedial timber treatment, re-roofing or spraying insecticides inside barns used to store grain. A Habitats Regulations licence will be required for work that would disturb bats or affect the roost. If you are unsure whether bats use the building, a survey should be conducted first. If bats are encountered during building or maintenance work, stop the work and call the SNCO immediately for advice. If they are unavailable call the National Bat Helpline or your local bat group.

Summary

	Use by bats		
	Roosting	**Foraging**	**Commuting**
Hedgerow management (no removal, maintenance, restoration, replanting, new planting, inter-planting, laying, coppicing, hedge bank restoration, buffer strips)	YES	YES	YES
Mature trees (retain and buffer hedgerow trees, in-field trees, waterside trees and dead wood)	YES	YES	
Farm woodland (retain, manage, plant new broadleaved, create linkages)	YES	YES	YES
Old orchards and parkland	YES	YES	
Farm buildings (retain roosts during restoration, sympathetic management)	YES		
Bat boxes	YES		
Arable buffer strips, uncropped field corners and beetle banks		YES	
Ditch, dyke and wetland retention, restoration, and management. Pond retention, creation and restoration. Buffer strips around ponds and streamside margins, exclude stock.		YES	YES
Hay meadows, wet meadows, meadow re-creation		YES	
Rotational set-aside (if not sprayed in the spring)		YES	
Arable reversion to grassland		YES	
Unimproved grassland, field margins of grasslands and pollen and nectar mixtures		YES	
Organic crops, conservation headlands, low-input, buffer zones,		YES	
Grazing (esp. cattle, esp. organic). Reduced use of avermectin anthelmintics.		YES	

Further reading

Anon. (2005) *Woodland management for bats.* Forestry Commission England and Wales, Bat Conservation Trust, Countryside Council for Wales and English Nature.

Entwistle A C, Harris S, Hutson A M, Racey P A, Walsh A, Gibson S D, Hepburn I and Johnston J (2001) *Habitat management for bats. A guide for land managers, land owners and their advisers.* JNCC, Peterborough.

Bat Conservation Trust (2003) *Agricultural practice and bats: A review of current research literature and management recommendations.* Defra Research Report BD2005.

English Nature (2003) *Managing landscapes for the greater horseshoe bat.* English Nature, Peterborough.

Mitchell-Jones A J and McLeish A P (eds) (2004) *Bat Workers Manual.* 3rd edition.

Further information

The Bat Conservation Trust runs the National Bat Helpline on 0845 1300 228, giving advice to callers about bats. Further information, including how to contact local bat groups, can be found on the Trust's website www.bats.org.uk.

5 Riverine mammals

5.1 Introduction

This chapter focuses on the conservation management of two species – the otter and the water vole. Both use a wide range of watercourses, large and small, still waters and wetlands. Water voles favour slower-flowing water with earth banks for burrowing and lush layered herbaceous vegetation to provide food and cover from predators. In wetlands they sometimes make nests in tall vegetation. They can travel overland between areas of habitat. Terrestrial habitat is equally important to otters for resting and for raising cubs, and they often travel overland. The otter is also found inhabiting suitable coastlines and estuaries, where it needs fresh water to clean the salt from its fur.

Otters are now widespread across most of the UK, so they should be considered in most places. In contrast, water voles have disappeared from many areas, and where they are present, they should be treated as high priority. The Local Wildlife Trust, Record Centre or Environment Agency may be able to provide information on distributions.

5.2 Otter

Population and distribution

Otters were once widespread in suitable habitat across the UK, but numbers were depressed by hunting, the loss and degradation of habitat, and pollution. Populations crashed in the late 1950s due to the agricultural use of toxic organochlorine pesticides. Though these were soon withdrawn from use, by the late 1970s otters were absent from much of the UK. The otter was given full legal protection in 1978. Since the 1980s, populations have slowly been recovering and this trend continues, though in many areas numbers have not fully recovered, and some parts still lack resident otters. Otters are more or less solitary, except a mother with cubs, and even where the population is healthy there will only be a few otters on a river.

David Kaer

Plate 5.1 Otter

Habitat requirements

Otters need areas with good food supplies (fish) and undisturbed places for resting, and females also require secure areas with dens for rearing cubs. A resident otter occupies a well-defined stretch of river and associated habitats including side streams, ditches, ponds, wetlands and woodlands, known as its 'home range'. It will get to know its home range, including good feeding places and safe resting sites, and will find novel features, eg a new pond. The size of an otter's home range will vary depending on what food is available and the presence of neighbouring otters.

A female otter tends to favour tributary streams over the main river, and within her home range of 10–20 km of watercourse has a smaller 'core area' where she spends most time, especially when raising her cubs. The male is more likely to travel about its range, which can be 20–40 km or more, and may travel 10 km in a night, feeding on the move. He will spend more time on larger rivers, perhaps returning to the same part every few days. The use an otter makes of different parts of its range may also vary seasonally, according to available food and conditions. On coasts which have a rich food supply home ranges are much smaller, eg 1–2 km of shoreline plus associated coastal streams. In addition to resident otters there are non-breeding animals which do not have defined home ranges.

On average, an otter's diet is 80% fish (average size only 12 cm long), with the remainder made up of amphibians, crustaceans, and occasionally waterfowl, rabbits and small mammals. In spring frogs spawning at ponds may be eaten in large numbers. In freshwater areas otters generally feed nocturnally and rest during the day.

Resting sites

An otter makes use of an undefined number of resting sites about its home range, to sleep in during the day and for short rests at night. Some may be used regularly, others only occasionally. Resting sites include above-ground shelter in bramble and other dense undergrowth, piles of woody flood debris, hollow trees and in reedbeds. In undisturbed areas an otter may just lie up in tall herbaceous

Plate 5.2 Eastburn Beck

vegetation. Underground resting sites or 'holts' include cavities amongst tree roots, enlarged rabbit burrows, badger setts, caves and dry drainage pipes. An otter may even rest in or under a shed or amongst piled timber. Resting sites are often difficult to identify, though sometimes they are marked with spraint (droppings) at or inside the entrance. They are generally near the water's edge, though not invariably so. Females tend to select particularly undisturbed locations, especially when accompanied by cubs.

Breeding areas

A female otter gives birth to one to five cubs (usually two or three), at any time of year. Cubs are born helpless and only venture out of their natal (breeding) den at about three months, after weaning has begun. The family group gradually ventures further afield within the mother's home range, and for a further 10 months or so the cubs learn the skills to hunt and become independent. They then disperse to seek their own home ranges. The male plays no part in rearing the young.

The breeding area is a key habitat requirement for otters. This is an area of land (or land plus open water) that is free from disturbance, where there is access to a good food supply and no risk of flooding. The area includes one or more potential natal den sites. The main habitat types used (as currently known) are extensive areas of scrub, deciduous woodlands, young conifer plantations, reed beds, ponds and lakes. Where good quality areas are unavailable sub-optimal ones will be used. A breeding area can be on any part of a river system but is more likely to be away from large rivers.

A natal den is a space similar to an ordinary resting site (see above), where the cubs are born and stay for up to three months. The cubs may be moved to different dens during this period, if the breeding area provides a choice of suitable sites. Natal dens may also be used which are not associated with an obvious breeding area. Natal dens are particularly difficult to identify, though potential sites may be found.

Cover and disturbance

The type, levels and proximity of disturbance tolerated by otters is unclear and varies between animals. However, it is likely to relate to the quality of bank-side cover (bank-side scrub and tall herbaceous vegetation) and resting sites available. Thus, where disturbance is very low otters can inhabit areas with very little cover. However, a resting otter is more likely to tolerate disturbance nearby if there is good cover on or near the river bank, eg dense scrub, tall herbaceous vegetation (available in the summer) or more substantial resting sites. Dogs off the lead may seek out an otter, so a regularly used bank top footpath is likely to cause more disturbance than some other types of activity eg fishing.

The level of disturbance accepted by a breeding female is likely to be low, but again this will depend on the individual and the quality of the habitat. If secure underground dens are available some disturbance in the wider area may be tolerated, whereas even low levels of disturbance may prevent breeding if only above ground den sites are present. Young cubs in the natal den may be found and killed by dogs whilst the mother is away feeding. They are particularly vulnerable where the den is in above-ground cover such as scrub.

Factors affecting populations of otters on lowland farmland

Accidental death
The main known cause of death is on the roads, eg at the type of road bridge where otters cannot easily travel along the watercourse beneath, or where a road passes between areas of habitat. Otters also die of blood poisoning from injuries caused by other otters and dogs.

Prey availability
Pollutants including farm waste, nutrient and sediment run-off, insecticides and herbicides affect the otters' fish and amphibian prey. River and bank vegetation management can damage fish habitats. Eel numbers are in steep decline.

Habitat loss, degradation and disturbance
Potential breeding areas and resting sites are lost through management of riverbanks, woodland etc, through land use change, and due to increased disturbance by people and dogs. Grazing of watercourse banks restricts the growth of scrub and tall herbaceous vegetation cover.

Himalayan balsam
In many places Himalayan balsam an invasive non-native annual plant, now dominates the vegetation on the banks of watercourses, ponds and lakes. It is shallow rooted and dies back in the autumn, leaving bare banks devoid of cover for otters and vulnerable to erosion.

5.3 Water vole

Population and distribution

The water vole was once widespread throughout Britain, but has been in gradual decline since 1900. Water voles have disappeared from 89% of surveyed sites since the 1980s. This decline in range and population density is continuing.

Habitat requirements

Water voles are found on almost any kind of waterway. They usually favour slow-flowing water where the level does not vary greatly. Water voles need banks that they can tunnel into to form burrow systems. Where water levels fluctuate, water voles prefer a high and steep or stepped bank profile so that they can tunnel upwards to remain above the water table in the bank. Although they prefer watercourses which flow throughout the year they will inhabit winterbournes and ditches which dry out. They generally use habitat within 3 m of the water edge, but burrow entrances have been found up to 10 m away and it is unknown how far underground burrow systems may extend. They can also use water meadows and wetlands if they have tussocks of grass, rush, sedge or reed in which water voles can create nests above the water table. Greater tussock sedge is particularly favoured. Sites that flood for protracted periods in winter are unsuitable, unless they offer nest sites above the flood water level. Estuaries and brackish water are generally avoided by water voles.

Water voles are herbivorous, and 227 species of plants have been identified in their diet. These include tall grasses, willowherb, loosestrife, meadowsweet and nettles on the river bank as well as reeds, sedges and rushes in the marginal vegetation. During the winter they may eat roots and strip bark from young willow shoots along the water edge. Water voles can climb and in early spring may eat young blackthorn leaves and hawthorn flowers. The amount of aquatic and bank vegetation is extremely important, and a mixture of species ensures a balanced diet and a supply of food throughout the year.

Aubrey Jenkins

Plate 5.3 Water vole

Plate 5.4 Everingham Beck

They prefer a continuous swathe of luxuriant layered growth, preferably at least 2 m wide at the water's edge. Sites excessively shaded by trees or scrub are generally not suitable.

Water voles are quite tolerant of disturbance and poor water quality. They are often found in urban situations. They may survive in these degraded habitats because fewer predators occur. Improving vegetation cover can enhance these sites.

Causes of decline

Habitat loss and degradation
On lowland farms, heavy grazing of the bank by livestock removes water voles' food and cover, exposing them to increased predation. Excessive trampling of the riverbank also collapses water vole burrows and damages the river profile, making the site unsuitable. Ploughing right up to the water channel and spraying vegetation at the river margin destroys water vole habitat. Artificial banks may prevent water voles burrowing into the bank and reduce the amount of marginal vegetation which water voles require for food and cover from predators. Frequent cutting will also reduce the riparian vegetation and make the habitat unsuitable for water voles.

Population fragmentation
Isolation of habitats and local extinction accelerates the rate of local decline. Isolated populations are particularly vulnerable to extinction in years of low breeding success. Water voles will disperse up to 1 km (or rarely up to 3 km) from their natal habitat along a watercourse. In some cases they will disperse across land, particularly where there are few barriers to dispersal such as roads.

Variations in water level
Excessive water level fluctuations can cause difficulties for water voles by flooding burrows and affecting access to food and cover. Where water levels are variable, voles prefer steep river banks. During floods, they must find high banks or unaffected backwater areas. A lack of such refuges may be a limiting factor on an otherwise ideal site. Flood defence engineering, land drainage and abstraction all affect the pattern and extent of fluctuations. Drying of streams and rivers, through over-abstraction of water, is also detrimental, as water voles are more vulnerable to terrestrial predators such as stoats and weasels.

Predation
Water voles normally live in balance with their natural predators such as weasels, stoats and otters. However, they are particularly vulnerable to the introduced American mink. The female mink is slim enough to enter the water vole's burrow and so pursue it both in the water and underground. Where habitat is good, with diverse vegetation and off-river ponds, ditches or wetlands, the impact of mink appears to be reduced. Urban situations seem to cause more disturbance to predators than to water voles, and they may sometimes survive on heavily disturbed waterways even in poor habitat.

Although rats do not in general predate water voles they do compete for burrow space along watercourses. They will kill water voles, particularly young, and some colonies of rats may occupy a large stretch of bank which may affect movement of water voles along watercourses.

Pollution
The effects of agricultural pollutants, such as farm waste, insecticides, herbicides and sheep dips, on water voles are not well known but may affect their breeding success.

Poisoning
Accidental killing during control of rats, rabbits or moles may be responsible for local extinction. There are methods of rat control which can be used in areas inhabited by water voles (see below).

5.4 Management advice

Managing for both otters and water voles

First check for the presence of otters and water voles and areas they may be using before starting any management which may disturb them or damage their habitats (this would be a criminal offence under the Wildlife and Countryside Act 1981), and to enable management of suitable areas to be tailored to their requirements. Otters are now present in much of the country and are likely to be using your land and water or be nearby without your knowledge. Water vole presence is very variable across the country so it may be necessary to have a survey carried if you are unsure if they are present.

If either otters or water voles are found to be present or nearby it is always important to consider including them in habitat management plans. Although their habitat needs differ it is possible to cater for both on a farm scale. Otters do not need continuous riverbank cover, but benefit from regular resting sites, and the provision of potential breeding areas every 5–10 km of river. Water vole habitat can be provided in between. The aim should be to provide a mosaic of habitats which together are beneficial to both species, including riverbanks, ponds, ditches and other wetland habitats.

Where water voles are present or nearby, management of existing or creation of new habitat for them in suitable locations should take priority. Habitat for otters can be located in places which will not compromise the needs of the water voles. Some areas such as watercourses with

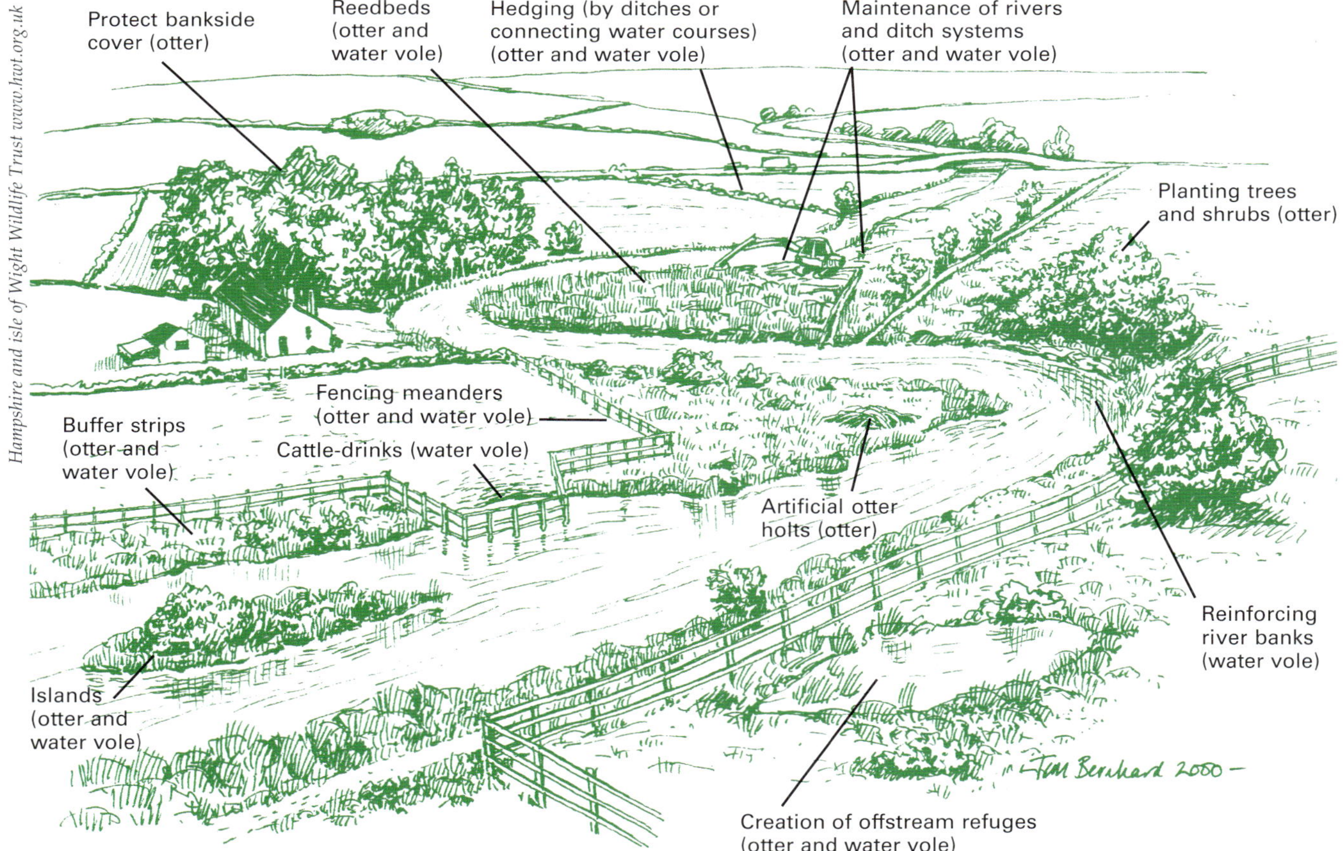

Figure 5.1
Habitat creation and management examples where otter and water vole are present.

Plate 5.5 Cattleholmes Foston Beck

rocky banks or fast flows are suitable for otters but not water voles.

How to manage for both species

- Maintain suitable banks to provide water vole habitat, but retain or plant trees and scrub for otters in small patches beyond the bank top, on a north bank (to minimise shading), in riverside field corners or meanders. Willow, hawthorn and crab apple all provide winter food for water voles.
- Buffer strips provide food for water voles and cover for both species. They can also intercept pollution and the roots of taller vegetation helps protect riverbanks against erosion, which benefits fish populations.
- Manage or create ponds with water vole habitat. Include an island or segment of the bank with scrub for otters – a holt can be installed. Amphibian ponds will provide a food supply for otters.

Peter Creed

Plate 5.6 Himalayan balsam

- In wetlands, retain or encourage some undisturbed areas of dense scrub for otters – islands are particularly good sites to install an artificial holt – and provide suitable banks, for water voles, especially on islands without otter holts.
- Control Himalayan balsam where it threatens to dominate the vegetation on watercourse and pond banks, to benefit both species.

Management to benefit otters

The highest priorities are to protect and maintain confirmed and potential breeding areas and resting sites, and management to benefit wild native fish populations. More general vegetation cover for otters along watercourse banks, around other habitat and along corridors between them is also beneficial, though not essential to otter survival. Always ensure that suitable habitat is not being used by otters before any management is carried out – seek expert advice.

Breeding areas

- Protect confirmed and potential breeding areas from destruction, damage and disturbance. Enhance sub-optimal sites (eg encourage or plant scrub, create an amphibian pond, build an artificial holt). Aim to protect the entire area.
- If necessary, manage confirmed or potential breeding habitat to maintain its value (eg coppice scrub in rotation if it becomes thin and leggy). Create potential natal dens to replace structures with a limited lifespan (eg hollow tree trunks).
- Create potential breeding areas in parts of a river catchment where they are scarce, or near to existing sites with a limited lifespan (eg young conifer plantation). They need to be near to a likely good food supply, free from flooding, be undisturbed and have potential natal dens (eg dense scrub, reedbed, log pile holts).
- Avoid creating breeding areas where otters are likely to be vulnerable to traffic (eg near a road bridge or culvert that is impassable to otters at high water, at a watershed that is bisected by a road, where otters are likely to cross a road to reach a feeding site).

Where this threat cannot be avoided, mitigation measures may be possible (eg otter underpass, bolt-on bridge ledges, otter fencing).

- Do not create a breeding area within 10 km of a fish farm or stocked lake unless the fishery owner has been consulted and they accept likely losses of fish to otters or will put up otter-proof fencing.

Management to benefit fish populations

Land management for otters should include work to protect and enhance wild native fish populations, their main prey.

- Minimise polluting run-off getting into watercourses, wetlands and ponds, including sediment.
- Plant or maintain bankside trees so that overhanging branches allow insects (fish prey) to drop into the water (preferably on the north bank to minimise shading).
- Retain in-channel woody debris since this provides habitat for fish and their invertebrate prey.

Creation and management of resting sites and cover

- Maintain, enhance or create areas of cover and resting sites on or connected to riverbanks, and on wetlands (eg fence cover from livestock, plant scrub in a field corner or inside a meander, where scrub is tall and leggy, coppice in rotation to regenerate dense cover at ground level).
- Retain patches of dense scrub, including in reedbeds, grassland, woodland, particularly where connected to watercourses or beside open water.
- Plant suitable trees on bank tops (eg oak, ash) to become root cavity holts in the future. Coppice or pollard badly leaning riverbank trees with existing holts to prevent them falling. Beware – a large tree or limb may be hollow with a natal den inside.
- Retain woody flood debris on river banks. Where this is not possible move timber to a suitable location nearby and construct a log pile holt. Where natural resting sites are scarce, construct an artificial log pile or 'pipe and chamber' holts in a quiet area.
- Rhododendron, laurel or Japanese knotweed thickets provide good cover for otters and may provide vital cover in breeding areas. Carry out control of these alien species in stages, replacing with native scrub.

Helen Taylor

Plate 5.7 Otter

- Protect areas of habitat from disturbance and route new access away from habitat, especially breeding areas. Avoid public access along both banks of a watercourse or around a pond.

Woodland management

Woodland is readily used by otters, and isolated woods may provide the best habitat in an intensive agricultural landscape. However mature woodlands with sparse ground cover are often of little value for otters.

- Create a widespread scrub layer within existing woodland (eg by coppice management) and provide potential natal den sites (eg a clearing with dense scrub – 10 × 10 m recommended minimum area – especially bramble, dog-rose or gorse. Ideally, they should be within a few metres of water, including very small streams and ditches).
- Construct log-pile holts from thinnings. Avoid stacking timber near a watercourse since it may be used as a resting site.

Management to benefit water voles

Creating buffer strips alongside watercourses

Buffer strips provide both corridors for

Andrew Dore

Plate 5.8 Water vole

movement and a diverse habitat for wildlife. Some specialised species, such as the water vole, are very heavily dependent on the quality of this buffer strip area. Buffer strips also reduce pollution and help protect riverbanks against erosion, by improving the binding of soil and bank by plant and tree roots. They reduce land run-off by increasing infiltration of rainwater into soils and serve to trap sediment from tilled fields before it enters the watercourse.

Plate 5.9 Harswell Beck buffer strip

The preferred width of buffer strips for water voles is not fixed. However, a margin of 6 m or more that supports a diverse range of plants undoubtedly benefits water voles by providing year-round food and cover. Unsprayed zones alongside watercourses, particularly when using Local Environmental Risk Assessment for Pesticides (LERAP) category A and B chemicals, help to improve water quality for wildlife. LERAP requirements provide the minimum standards of buffering required. Restoration and enhancement to link up suitable areas of habitat adjacent to existing colonies and creating stepping stones such as a series of ponds between colonies separated by unsuitable habitat will help the survival of local populations.

Cutting, strimming and mowing weeds

Regular cutting of vegetation along waterways can pose a serious problem for water voles by removing both food supply and concealment from predators. This is particularly serious when this is done over long lengths and at frequent time intervals. Where cutting of water weed is necessary, leave at least half of the channel uncut if possible. If vegetation management on the riverbank is deemed necessary (eg to prevent scrub development) it should be done on short stretches using as long a rotation period as possible. Create buffer strips at least 2 m wide, and manage as follows:

- Cut only one bank in a particular year and leave a fringe of vegetation at the water's edge.
- Cut vegetation in a patchwork of alternating strips no greater than 50 m long in a two- or three-year rotation. If there is no need to cut to ground level, set the cutting height to the highest possible setting. A cutting height of 15 cm will ensure water voles have some useful cover. Remove or pile up cuttings to prevent them killing the vegetation underneath.
- Consider the timing of vegetation management carefully. Ideally, where alternative patches of vegetation are to be left standing, it is best to delay cutting until breeding has finished in late autumn. If standing vegetation cannot be left it is better to cut the vegetation before mid-September, so that it can recover to some extent before

the end of the growing season. In this case, leaving a minimum of 15 cm cut height is very important.

- Avoid areas supporting dense colonies of water voles or give these areas special small-scale treatment.

Bankside grazing, fencing and hedging
Fencing or hedging can solve problems caused by grazing. Left unchecked, grazing causes similar problems to mowing bankside vegetation (see above). Fencing set back from the bank allows a suitable, diverse river bank flora to develop. A mosaic of a species-rich grassy sward and scrub encourages the greatest diversity of wildlife. Periodic limited access by livestock to the fenced area controls scrub encroachment. Access may be required for flood defence machinery. Drinking bays in the fencing allow livestock access to water in a controlled way. Alternatively, hedges can be used as fencing and provide additional habitat and food for water voles and other species, providing that they do not shade out the marginal and aquatic vegetation. Hedges should be broad at the base to provide good cover, and maintained on a rotational basis to provide a range of different ages. Some saplings can be allowed to grow into mature trees. Willow, hawthorn and crab apple all provide winter foods for water voles.

- Fence or part-fence the bank to provide refuges for water voles. Suitable meanders may be fenced off permanently. This allows natural regeneration and retention of water vole habitat using the minimum of materials.
- Electric fencing can be used to provide temporary exclusion. The fencing can be moved to allow stock periodic access to prevent encroachment of scrub in areas where water vole habitat is being encouraged.
- Where no fencing is provided, stocking densities should be reduced and vigilance to bank damage and adjustment of stocking density accordingly is essential.

De-silting
Well-managed ditches can be vital sanctuaries for water voles. Water vole habitat is enhanced by reducing the frequency of de-silting and vegetation cutting, and by managing water levels to ensure a permanent supply throughout the year.

Plate 5.10
Alternate bank cut

- Work short stretches at a time in rotation. At least one third of the ditch should remain untouched in any year. Leave gaps of 20–30 m as refuges where water voles occur.
- When de-silting, work from one bank and as far back from the water's edge as possible to minimise compacting and trampling of habitat. Take care to avoid damaging any burrows especially along the water line and retain the vegetation margins. Dispose of spoil carefully, avoiding spraying the banks in mud and site the spoil at least 2 m away from the bank. Storing overnight will let the spoil drain and may allow some mobile animals to crawl back into the water. Work should be done in winter.
- Work upstream to allow seeds and invertebrates to return to the disturbed length downstream.

Reinforcing of river banks
River banks can be reinforced in ways that improve water vole habitat. Some bank erosion may be acceptable as a natural process. The Environment Agency (England and Wales), Scottish Environment Protection Agency (SEPA) or Department of Environment (Northern Ireland, DoE (NI)) can advise on the likelihood of erosion becoming a serious problem, and on the various 'soft

engineering' techniques available, such as pre-planted coir fibre rolls or willow logs on shallow slopes and faggots and spiling on higher banks. The use of steel piling, rock gabion baskets, masonry or cement bags should be avoided wherever possible. Consents may be required from the Environment Agency, SEPA or DoE (NI) to install bank protection. Even where no water voles occur, unsympathetic reinforcement will prevent future spread of the species along the river.

Rat control

Rats may compete with and even prey on water voles, therefore where both species occur together rat control may be beneficial to water voles. However, pest control can lead to the unnecessary destruction of water vole colonies. Water voles may be mistaken for rats, or may be killed through indiscriminate control methods.

- Always survey for water voles before controlling rats along waterways.
- Avoid the use of poison where water voles occur. Do not block or place poison inside burrows. It is illegal to block or obstruct water vole burrows. If correct identification is in doubt, do not use poison, or seek the advice of a professional ecologist. Where no alternative is feasible, poison should be covered or enclosed in a bait box. This should be placed at least 5 m from the waterway preferably away from long vegetation, as rats are more likely to cross an open space than are water voles. Avoid the use of poisoned grain or pellets – use wax or soap blocks instead. If possible, raise the bait off the ground, as rats are more likely to climb than water voles.
- Avoid the use of back-break or snap traps. If used, these should be placed at least 5 m from the waterway. Live capture cage traps are the only safe option – check twice per day to release non-target species. Position traps in the open rather than in dense vegetation. Avoid placing traps at the water's edge.
- Regularly inspect and monitor pest control sites, clearing away poisoned corpses. If any dead water voles are found, review the control method used.

Mink control

Consideration should be given to controlling mink on important sites where water voles occur. Mink will almost certainly return from outside the trapped area, and such control should be considered as long-term management. Control should be carried out humanely using live-capture traps. This is an efficient proven method and non-target animals, such as juvenile otters and polecats, may be released unharmed. Otter guards can be fitted to the front of cages. The most effective time to do this is August–April, during the mating season. The use of mink hounds should be avoided, as it causes extreme levels of disturbance to habitats and to wildlife, particularly to otters and nesting birds.

The Game Conservancy Trust have developed mammal tracking rafts, which can be used to ascertain whether mink are passing through an area. The rafts contain a moist clay plate and are positioned next to the watercourse bank, which is the habitat that mink most frequently pass through. The mink walk over the plate, and it can be checked on a weekly basis for footprints. When mink footprints are found, a live-capture trap can be placed on the raft and any mink dispatched when caught. The rafts are labour-saving compared to bank side traps as they only require checking once a week using the clay plate (checks need to be carried out twice a day when live-capture traps are placed on the raft) and they have been found to be extremely effective at removing all the mink from watercourses. The Environment Agency, SEPA or DoE (NI) should be consulted before rafts are placed along watercourses to avoid obstructing any structures such as bridges and weirs.

- Use only live capture traps. Position bankside traps firmly on flat ground and restrain securely to stop any rolling into the water. Use stakes or trees to secure rafts to the banks. Ensure the bankside trap is above the level of rising water.
- Site bankside traps along linear features, such as hedges or walls, or near features such as weirs, old pollarded trees or under bridges. Mink rafts should be

David Kjaer

Plate 5.11 American mink

sited near areas of scrub and woodland and away from fast-moving water close to structures in the water. Do not set traps near any potential otter holt, such as exposed tree roots or stick piles (this is illegal).

- Avoid placing bankside traps and rafts in the open where they may be found by passers-by, or interfered with by livestock or badgers.
- Traps should be wrapped in hay, which a mink will pull inside and create a nest in when caught. This reduces the stress of the trapped animal, and provides a visual indication of a capture. Rafts should be covered with local vegetation to make them more inviting to mink passing by.
- Bait the trap with sardines or day old chick carcasses. Rafts do not require baiting as they are generally revisited by mink.
- Check the live-capture traps twice daily, at first light and late afternoon. Obtain a positive identification of a trapped animal before dealing with it. Dispatch caught mink cleanly. Specialist advice is available from the Game Conservancy Trust. Drowning is not an acceptably humane method of killing. It is illegal to release a mink back into the wild, once caught. Grey squirrels, brown rats, ferrets and polecat-ferrets should also be dispatched. Polecats are native to Britain and should be released unharmed.

Further reading

Crawford A (2003) *Fourth otter survey of England 2000–2002*. Environment Agency.

Environment Agency (1999) *Otters and river habitat management* (2nd edition). Environment Agency.

Liles G (2003) *Enhancing the status of the otter.* Conserving Natura 2000 Rivers Conservation Techniques Series No. 5. English Nature, Peterborough.

Quine C, Shore R and Trout R (eds) (2004) *Managing woodlands and their mammals*. Forestry Commission.

Strachan R and Moorhouse T (2006) *Water vole conservation handbook. Second edition*. Wildlife Conservation Research Unit, Oxford.

Water Vole Steering Group (1997) *Species Action Plan for the United Kingdom – water vole* Arvicola terrestris. DoE/EA.

Summary of habitat management advice

	Otter	Water vole
Ditch management	✔	✔
Hedgerow management close to water	✔	✔
Buffering in-field ponds	✔	✔
Buffer strips along field margins in grassland and arable land (useful between and along watercourses)	✔	✔
Field corner management (such as the inside of a meander loop)	✔	✔
Conservation headlands (along a watercourse or around a pond)	✔	✔
Maintenance of designed and traditional/engineered water bodies (such as millponds where these have a natural bank)	✔	✔
Maintenance, restoration and creation wet grassland	✔	✔
Creation of inter-tidal and saline habitat	✔	✔
Maintenance and creation of ponds	✔	✔
Maintenance, restoration and creation of reedbeds and fens	✔	✔
Rotational scrub management	✔	
Retain old/mature trees with hollow trunks	✔	
Pollard riverside trees to extend their lifespan	✔	
Create a thick shrub layer in woodlands using coppicing/edge management	✔	
Leave lying timber or construct a log-pile holt	✔	
Uncropped, cultivated margins on arable land (along a watercourse)		✔
Permanent or temporary fencing and management to stop the development of scrub		✔
Mink control and rat control		✔

6 Seed-eating birds

6.1 Introduction

Many of the bird species that depend on arable or mixed farmland are largely dependent on seed food, particularly through the winter. They include the grey partridge, pigeons and doves, skylark, sparrows, finches and buntings. Some are dependent on seed food throughout their lifecycle (eg linnet), whilst others are dependent on insect food as chicks and may take insects as adults when available in the summer (eg corn bunting). Many of these species have declined since the 1970s, partly due to the reduction in the availability of seed food on farmland, but also in some cases due to declines in insect numbers, changes in crops grown and timing of sowing. In this chapter, we concentrate on the farmland species that have declined, and are therefore the focus of conservation effort through agri-environment schemes. Conservation effort is most likely to be successful for a particular species if undertaken within about 2 km of sites where the species is known to occur, as these species are generally site-faithful and have small home ranges.

6.2 Populations and distributions

There is a general distinction between seed-eating birds that are dependent on farmland habitats, which have declined by more than 50% since the 1970s (eg tree sparrow and yellowhammer), and seed-eating birds that can also utilise other habitats such as woodland and gardens, which have increased or remained stable (eg greenfinch and chaffinch). There are also a few seed-eating species that are not dependent on farmland that have declined seriously (eg house sparrow in urban and rural habitats, and redpoll in woodlands).

Roger Wilmshurst/rspb-images.com

Plate 6.1 Yellowhammer

Chris Gomersall/rspb-images.com

Plate 6.2 Cirl bunting There has been a dramatic recovery of one species, the rare cirl bunting in Devon. Here specialist advice and agri-environment scheme funding was targeted at farms within the breeding range and resulted in a very high proportion of farms with the bird undertaking suitable management. This example shows how appropriate farm management can reverse the declines of seed-eating birds.

Causes of decline

Despite being a group of species with similar foraging habitat requirements, there is not simply a single cause of decline of seed-eating species on farmland. These species forage in a variety of ways, and there is a different emphasis on the importance of summer and winter food provision in relation to the cause of decline. Indeed, there is rarely a single cause of decline for any one species. It is often a combination of two or more factors. Table 6.1 lists the main factors identified by research.

6.3 Habitat requirements

The three basic habitat requirements of seed-eating birds on farmland are nesting habitat, summer foraging habitat and winter foraging habitat. Many farmland species, notably partridge, skylark and the buntings, favour open farm landscapes and avoid areas enclosed by buildings, woodland or tall hedgerows. Provision of habitats for these species should be focused on the more open landscapes of the farm.

Nesting habitat is rarely regarded as a limiting factor for these species (with the exception of the skylark), as most of the declines are attributed to shortages of insect or seed food. However, it is worth checking that appropriate nesting habitat is present for the species concerned. Nesting habitat can be provided for most of these species through good management of field boundary and field margins habitats, notably tall thick hedgerows (turtle dove), shorter hedgerows with grass margins (linnet, yellowhammer and cirl bunting) and tussocky grass margins or beetle banks (grey partridge). The tree

Table 6.1 Causes of decline of seed-eating birds.

Species	Causes of decline
Grey partridge	Increased pesticide use (loss of insect food) and predation
Turtle dove	Loss of summer seed food and tall scrub
Skylark	Loss of spring cropping and improvement of grasslands
Tree sparrow	Loss of seed and insect food on farmland
Linnet	Loss of summer seed food
Yellowhammer	Loss of winter seed food and rough grassland, and increased pesticide use (affecting insect food abundance)
Cirl bunting	Loss of winter seed food, rough grassland areas and mixed farming
Reed bunting	Loss of winter seed food and damp habitats
Corn bunting	Loss of winter seed food and increased use of pesticides (and possibly nest destruction during harvesting)

Chris Gomersall/rspb-images.com

Andy Hay/rspb-images.com

Plate 6.3 (left) Linnet

Plate 6.4 (right) Tree sparrow

sparrow is a hole-nesting bird, which can occupy holes in mature trees or farm buildings, or can take up nestboxes. The skylark, reed bunting and corn bunting generally nest in the crops or grassland. Modern arable crops are generally well suited to nesting reed and corn buntings, although a fair proportion of reed bunting nests in oilseed rape and corn bunting nests generally are still active at harvest time. Some nests can be protected by use of later harvested crops, and avoiding swathing of oilseed rape crops. In the case of skylark, the height and density of winter-sown crops and the frequency of cutting of silage meadows are issues that needs specific mitigation.

Birds require food to be both abundant and accessible. For these species, this generally means availability of food on the ground where they forage. In addition, grey partridge and, to a lesser extent, skylark and corn bunting, need cover to protect them from predators. Standing arable crops can provide both protective cover from predators and access to the ground for most of these species.

The key invertebrate groups taken by seed-eating birds in the spring and summer are grasshoppers, caterpillars, beetles, flies and sawflies. Spiders are also important in the diet of skylarks and the buntings, bugs (including aphids) are important for grey partridges, skylarks and tree sparrows, and dragonflies are important for reed buntings. Grasshoppers and caterpillars are largely found in margin habitats.

Dragonflies are obviously associated with wetland habitats and watercourses. Spiders, beetles, flies, sawflies and aphids are generally taken from within the crops themselves, although most except the sawflies will overwinter in the hedgerows and tussocky grassland in field margins. Pollen and nectar mixtures can boost numbers of butterflies and moths. Good field margin management is important for boosting numbers of key insect groups, but low-input crop management is also important for providing insects in areas where they are more accessible. Grazed pasture can also be a good source of invertebrate food, particularly of phytophagous and dung-degrading insects.

In winter, they seek seed-rich habitats. The important plant groups are cereals and

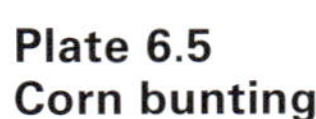
Plate 6.5 Corn bunting

Mark Hamblin/rspb-images.com

grass weeds for the buntings, and broadleaved weeds (notably polygonums, fat-hen and chickweed) and oilseed rape for the other species. All of the declining species apart from linnets will feed on any spilt cereal grain, either in stubbles, wild bird covers or farmyards. Unimproved pastures can provide seed food for these species, but the linnet is the only one of these species that can generally be found in a landscape without any arable farming.

The linnet and turtle dove are the exceptional species that feed on seeds throughout the year, and need an abundant seed source through the summer to feed their chicks. Areas with an abundance of broadleaved weeds are useful. In the case of turtle doves, open, accessible ground is required, as this large seed-eating bird cannot forage in dense crops or field margin vegetation. The dandelion is an important weed in grassland situations for these species.

During the summer, birds are dependent on food resources within easy reach of their nest sites, so insect-rich habitats within a few hundred metres of the nest site are far more valuable than small pockets elsewhere on the farm. As such, a network of insect-rich habitats around the farm makes the farm more accessible to nesting birds. Conversely, birds may range more widely in winter, so a few, large pockets of seed-rich habitats around the farm are likely to be just as successful as many small pockets.

6.4 Management advice

The objectives of management to conserve the suite of seed-eating birds should be to provide or enhance nesting opportunities, create a network of insect-rich habitats around the farm and ensure that there are adequate pockets of seed-rich habitats through the winter (and the summer for turtle doves and linnets). Field boundary nesting species should be adequately provided for by rotational hedgerow and ditch management outside of the nesting season (March–August inclusive), protection of isolated trees and areas of scrub, creating gradated edges to farm woodlands and maintaining nesting opportunities in farm buildings. A diversity of hedge sizes should be maintained in keeping with the landscape character, with short, thick hedges in open areas of the farm with large field sizes, and tall, thick hedges connecting areas of woodland or scrub, or in more enclosed areas of the farm. Other management to provide nesting and

David Kjaer

Plate 6.6
Grey partridge

feeding opportunities in the field margins and centres will differ between arable and grassland systems.

The Game Conservancy Trust estimate that good management for grey partridge can be achieved by providing 6.9 km of margin management and 5 ha of insect-rich chick-rearing cover per 100 ha. This amount of insect food provision should also accommodate the other species. A good winter food supply could be provided for them through 10 ha of stubble management or 1 ha of wild bird cover or unharvested crop per 100 ha.

Arable land

Tussocky grass buffer strips will offer nesting habitat for grey partridges and overwintering habitat for a range of insects. Margins of watercourses can be managed to encourage aquatic insects (see Chapter 10, dragonflies). On large-scale arable systems with fields greater than 16 ha, beetle banks with tussocky grassland can be created through the middle of fields to boost insect abundance and partridge nesting opportunities. Margins with a wildflower component or strips of pollen and nectar mixtures (a mix of legumes flowering consecutively through the summer) will boost numbers of pollinating insects.

On lighter soils, cereals can be managed without the use of herbicides that remove broadleaved weeds or summer insecticides to boost in-field insect abundance directly. Grass weed herbicides and fungicides are still applied, and fertilisers can be used as normal, although added benefits for broadleaved plants accrue if fertiliser rates are dropped, and this can also reduce the build-up of aggressive weeds. This management can be restricted to the headlands (conservation headlands) or adopted on whole fields. Uncropped, cultivated margins or plots on lighter soils will also boost numbers of broadleaved weeds and the insects associated with them. This option can also provide an accessible seed source for turtle doves through the summer.

Winter seed-rich habitats can be created through retention of crop stubbles (eg using rotational set-aside) or the creation of unharvested standing crops. The value of winter stubbles largely depends on the abundance of seed-bearing weeds within them, which generally relates to the level of weed control in the preceding crop. Stubbles following low-input cereals or conservation headlands can be particularly beneficial. Seed crops can be retained through the winter by leaving conservation headlands unharvested or by establishing a mix of unharvested crops (or wild bird covers) every spring. Some of the components of these crops are biennial, in which case, they are left in the ground for two years to provide seed in the second winter.

Spring cropping is beneficial for most field-nesting species, and these crops often have lower inputs and therefore may have more weeds and insects. Rotational set-aside can be very useful, but if it is sprayed early in the breeding season, then the benefits for nesting birds and food supply are quickly lost. Skylark plots are particularly important for boosting in-field foraging opportunities in winter cereal fields through the summer in systems where the majority of crops are sown in the autumn and too dense in the spring for easy access to the ground.

David Tipling/rspb-images.com

Plate 6.7 Skylark

Andy Hay/rspb-images.com

Plate 6.8 Skylark plots

The benefits are proven for skylarks, but they may also benefit other species.

Grassland

Buffer strips can also be created in grass fields, most easily in hay and silage fields, where the strips can be left uncut. They are less likely to attract nesting grey partridges, but they will boost the abundance of some insects. It is important to leave these margins unfertilised, and uncultivated if grass leys are reseeded, as they should be allowed to develop a native grass sward.

The main limiting factor for seed-eating birds in grassland systems is the provision of seed food. Creation or maintenance of arable cropping for livestock feed, or mitigation through establishment of wild bird cover crops are the easiest ways of ensuring a supply of seed food. Where fodder crops are a possibility, low-inputs, spring sowing and retention of winter stubbles are all likely to boost the benefits. Fodder brassica crops that are strip grazed through the winter can provide particularly high numbers of weed seeds and attract large flocks of seed-eating birds. Some seed food can be provided by allowing broadleaved weeds to survive in grass leys or leaving the grass uncut and ungrazed towards the end of the growing season to go to seed.

Further reading

Anderson G Q A, Bradbury, R B and Evans A D (2001) *Evidence for the effects of agricultural intensification on wild bird populations in the UK*. RSPB Research Report No 3.

Vickery J A, Tallowin J R, Feber R E, Asteraki E J, Atkinson P W, Fuller R J and Brown V K (2001) The management of lowland neutral grasslands in Britain: effects of agricultural practices on birds and their food resources. *Journal of Applied Ecology* 38: 647–664.

Winspear R and Davies G (2005) *A management guide to birds of lowland farmland*. The RSPB, Sandy.

Summary

	Nesting	Insect food	Seed food
Hedgerow management and scrub maintenance	Turtle dove, linnet, yellowhammer, cirl bunting		
Mature trees, farm buildings and nestboxes	Tree sparrow		
Arable field margins, corners and beetle banks	Grey partridge	✔	
Ditch and wetland management	Reed bunting	✔	
Spring crops	Skylark, cirl bunting	✔	
Skylark plots and fixed set-aside	Skylark	✔	
Hay meadows	Skylark	✔	✔
Rotational set-aside	Skylark	?	✔
Unimproved grassland, field margins of grasslands and pollen and nectar mixtures		✔	
Organic crops, conservation headlands, low-input cereals and undersown spring cereals		✔	?
Cultivated margins and plots, wild bird cover crops		✔	✔
Over-wintered stubble, arable pockets in grassland areas, weed retention in grasslands			✔
✔ = positive benefits ? = Potential benefits depending on management and outcome			

7 Breeding waders of lowland farmland

7.1 Introduction

This chapter covers the conservation of lapwing, curlew, redshank and snipe on lowland wet grassland and of lapwing and stone-curlew on unimproved dry grassland and spring-sown arable crops. In general, these are target species for agri-environment scheme funding in the UK. Collectively, they require an abundant source of accessible soil and surface invertebrates and either grassland swards that provide them with nesting cover and suitable feeding habitat, or, in the case of lapwings and stone-curlews, spring-sown arable crops suitable for nesting. The chapter does not cover the rare or very localised populations of curlews nesting in arable crops, ringed plovers nesting in the Brecklands of East Anglia and black-tailed godwits nesting on wet grassland in the Fens.

Chris Gomersall/rspb-images

Plate 7.1 Curlew

7.2 Populations and distributions

The populations of all five species declined significantly during the 20th century, largely due to loss of suitable breeding habitat, particularly on lowland farmland. The snipe is now almost restricted to nature reserves as a nesting bird in lowland England and Wales but is still more widespread in Scotland and Northern Ireland. In the case of the rare stone-curlew, a population recovery started in the 1990s due to a combination of nest protection and habitat restoration through a project run by the RSPB in conjunction with farmers and landowners, using agri-environment scheme funding.

Causes of decline

The decline of these species has largely been due to the drainage and other agricultural improvement of wet grasslands, and loss of chalk grassland

Plate 7.2 (left) Redshank

Plate 7.3 (right) Stone-curlew

Chris Gomersall/rspb-images

Chris Gomersall/rspb-images

Andy Hay/rspb-images.com

Plate 7.4 Lapwing

and Breck heath in the case of the stone-curlew.

Wet grassland has largely been converted to improved grassland through drainage, increased use of inorganic fertilisers and reseeding. On these improved swards, the dense, fast-growing grass, combined with the increased stocking rates or a switch to silage production has discouraged nesting birds. Some has been cultivated for arable production and other areas have been abandoned and become unsuitable without the necessary grazing regime. Some areas have dried out as a result of drainage, water abstraction or modification of natural floodplains. Important coastal wetlands are now at risk from sea level rise. Remaining populations of breeding waders on lowland wet grassland are small due to the loss and fragmentation of this habitat. The numbers of lapwing, curlew, redshank and snipe are far greater in the uplands than in the small isolated populations left on lowland farmland.

Unimproved dry grasslands have been lost due to many of the same factors. In the case of lapwings and stone-curlews, the loss of mixed farming and spring-sown arable crops have further restricted the availability of nesting and feeding habitat.

Populations of these species are now often concentrated on small sites.

7.3 Habitat requirements

Breeding waders generally nest in large fields on open farmland and avoid areas close to woods, trees, tall hedges or inhabited areas. They are very site faithful, and management should always focus on areas with recent evidence of nesting within 2 km. Ideally, individual fields where nests have been seen in the past should be targeted for conservation.

Breeding success relates to the availability of soil and surface invertebrates, the sward structure, the levels of predation and disturbance, and the risks of agricultural operations or nest trampling by stock. On wet grassland, the accessibility of food to breeding waders is determined by the sward structure and the water level. Soil invertebrate accessibility is highest on peat soils when the water table is kept between 20 to 30 cm below the surface between mid-March and the end of June, particularly for snipe and curlew. On clay or silt soils, pools of surface water which gradually recede throughout this period are more likely to provide good feeding conditions, especially for redshank and lapwing.

Suitable wet grassland habitats can be found in:

- natural river floodplains where water levels rise through the winter and gradually recede through the spring
- washlands specifically created for the storage of flood water, which are prone to sudden inundation when water has to be diverted from main drains to maintain drainage of land at or below sea-level
- water meadows specifically designed in the 17th and 18th centuries to undergo controlled flooding to boost fertility of hay meadows – few remain in working order
- wetland areas and coastal grazing marshes on peat and alluvial soils, which have largely been drained and improved, but some, such as those in the Somerset Levels, have been restored as semi-natural habitats under agri-environment schemes or nature reserve management
- temporarily inundated grassland areas next to large, undisturbed water-bodies,

Andy Hay/rspb-images.com

Plate 7.5
Snipe

which can support wet grassland communities

- grassland next to shallow-sided drainage channels – these can support nesting birds in some circumstances.

In the lowlands, snipe are completely dependent on wet grassland for nesting and feeding during the breeding season, and redshanks use this or intertidal areas. Redshank breeding sites typically have areas of shallow water used for feeding through until at least June. Snipe use wet flushes with soft soil for probing for food. They can make use of wet flushes as small as 0.2 ha. They need to be able to feed close to the nest site, as the adults carry food to the chicks for a period after hatching. The lapwing and curlew also occupy this habitat, but can also make use of dry grassland and arable land, particularly the lapwing, which is the most numerous and widespread of the four on farmland. The strongholds of these four species are now in the relatively unimproved upland farm habitats, particularly wet areas of in-bye grassland.

The stone-curlew is restricted to mixed farmland with spring-sown arable crops or areas of unimproved dry grassland in central-southern England and the Brecklands of East Anglia. Here, its requirements are very similar to those of the lapwings nesting in the same area, namely large fields with an open vista and a short sward (less than 15 cm in spring-sown arable crops or less than 5 cm on chalk grassland or Breckland). It can rear two broods in a year, so has a relatively prolonged breeding season from early April, potentially running until mid-September.

Table 7.1 Requirements for breeding waders on wet grassland.

Species	Sward height	Soil/water condition	Breeding season
Lapwing	Short sward c5 cm with occasional tussocks on up to 10% of the area	Damp soil and edge of shallow water preferred for feeding	Mid-March–mid-July
Curlew	Intermediate: short areas for feeding and taller areas or tussocks (c20 cm) for nesting	Damp soil preferred for feeding	Early April–mid-July
Redshank	Intermediate: short areas (5–15 cm) for feeding and tussocks for nesting	Surface water essential	Early April–end of July
Snipe	Tall sward (>25 cm) for nesting and shorter areas (<10 cm) for feeding	Soft damp soil essential	Early April–mid-August

7.4 Management advice

All five species considered in this chapter require open habitats away from woodland, tall hedgerows, walls or trees. It is important to avoid planting new woods, trees or hedges, or allow existing hedges to grow significantly taller in areas used by breeding waders. Other areas of the farm may be better suited to these forms of habitat creation.

Wet grassland management and restoration for breeding waders

Management of wet grassland for nesting lapwing, curlew, redshank and snipe involves maintaining suitable sward structure (generally by grazing) to provide nesting cover and open feeding areas, and ensuring that high water levels or wet features are available to provide accessible soil invertebrate and surface insect food throughout the breeding season. Although each species has its own specific requirements (see above), management can accommodate all four within one area of wet grassland if the sward diversity provides the whole range of short grassland and tussocky areas across the field. Management can be tailored more closely on sites where only one or two of the species occur.

On existing sites, it is worth checking whether the optimal conditions are provided by the current management. On grazed sites, the stocking rate should be determined by the productivity of the sward. Between April and June, the minimum number of grazing animals should be used to maintain a suitable sward height and diversity. Whilst curlew and snipe may tolerate zero grazing during this period, redshank and lapwing will generally require some level of grazing to maintain the right sward height. Although cattle are considered to create a better sward structure than other livestock, in most cases the grazing regime is probably more important than the stock type.

Mechanical operations such as rolling, chain harrowing and topping should be avoided between mid-March and 1 July to prevent destruction of nests and young. On sites used by breeding waders that are cut for hay or silage, cuts should be delayed until after 15 July. Where not practical, leaving uncut areas around wet flushes will protect areas most likely to accommodate unfledged chicks.

High water levels (within 20–30 cm of the surface) or areas of shallow water (in shallow-sided ditches, foot drains, damp hollows or specifically created wader scrapes) should be maintained between March and June. It is useful to have control of the water levels to prevent fields drying

R Winspear (The RSPB)

Plate 7.6 Land restored to wet grassland, providing habitat for wintering wildfowl and breeding waders such as the lapwing, redshank and snipe.

out too early in dry springs or prolonged waterlogging in wet summers. Sluices in drainage channels can be used to raise and control water levels (Figure 7.1).

The soil should not be saturated for prolonged periods. If controllable, the water table should be lowered in July to allow at least a four-month dry period to allow heavier grazing and mechanical management of the sward. Late summer is the ideal time to graze the sward right down to provide suitable conditions in the following spring. Grazing during autumn or winter might be necessary where there is significant grass growth during winter.

Rush infestations are a common problem on wet grasslands. They can reduce the productivity of the sward, and may lead to abandonment of grazing on some sites. They also create a dense tall sward that is unsuitable for nesting waders, at least for lapwings and redshanks. Management should be considered when levels exceed 30% of the field area. It should be undertaken after chicks have fledged, or in August if the timing of breeding cannot be determined. Cutting and removing the rushes as low as possible, but without scalping the ground, is a good first step in management. This can be followed by a second cut 4–8 weeks later, aftermath grazing (but take care not to poach the ground) or applying MCPA or glyphosate with a weed wiper to the regrowth when it is higher than the rest of the sward.

Grazed wet grassland should not require any inputs of fertiliser above the fertility provided by the grazing stock. It is not appropriate to use any inorganic fertiliser or slurry. Organic manure, such as farmyard manure should not be applied at rates above 25t/ha/yr. Avermectins are commonly used to worm stock, but they can have a detrimental impact on the dung fauna, which is an important invertebrate food source. Their use can be reduced by using rotational or mixed grazing regimes, not treating all stock at the same time or using alternatives when stock are grazing important fields for nesting waders.

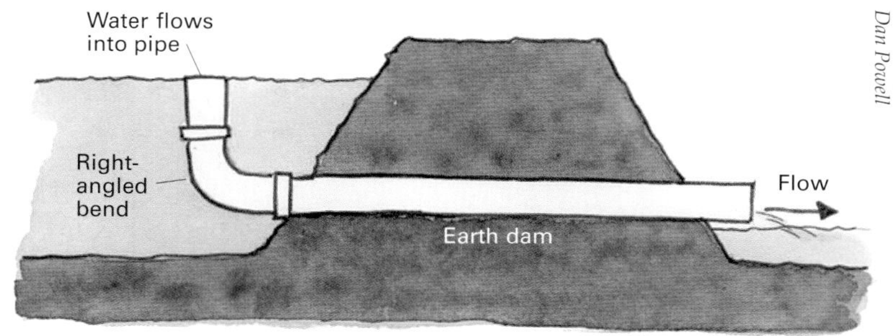

Figure 7.1
Diagram of a pipe sluice. Bunds need to be carefully engineered so that they are stable and impervious. Construction is easier in areas with loamy or clay soils and bunds should be keyed into an impermeable substrate. They should extend well into the bank on each side to reduce seepage losses and gentle profiles are advisable to enable mowing of any colonising rank vegetation. If a bund is necessary, aim to locate it appropriately within the landscape.

Creation of wet grasslands for breeding waders

Arable reversion to wet grassland or re-wetting grasslands requires careful thought and planning. Success is more likely where the site has suitable hydrological conditions, and is adjacent to existing wet grassland. Arable reversion should only be attempted on soils with a low nutrient status (eg phosphorus level of one or below). A plentiful source of clean water (not tap water) is essential. The area of land affected by raising the water level needs to be considered. Will it affect neighbouring areas of land where high water levels are not desirable?

Before creating a grass sward, it is worth manipulating the topography to ensure that wet and dry areas can be accommodated on the site after re-wetting. Application of farmyard manure may be useful in raising the organic matter content of the soil.

Eventually, re-wetting can be achieved by removing or blocking field drains, using sluices in drainage ditches or creating new wet features within the field, such as wader scrapes. Maintaining high ditch levels will ensure a high in-field water table on peaty soils, but less likely on clay soils – surface irrigation or the creation of wet features are more likely to be needed here. The aim should be to maintain a high water table over 30% of the area, or standing water on

G Woodburn (The RSPB)

Plate 7.7 A small, newly created scrape.

5–10% of the area throughout the period from March to early June). Wet grassland management as described above should then be adopted.

Wader scrapes can be used to provide a source of aquatic invertebrate prey and provide accessible soil invertebrates around the edges. They should be designed to hold water from March to late June. They should be located at least 100 m from field boundary features such as hedgerows and trees, and away from overhead wires. Do not create them in areas of high floristic interest or diversity, or in seasonally wet areas and areas of damp peat, that can be important for their existing invertebrate fauna (at least check with specialists first. You can get important wet ground invertebrates on botanically-poor areas). The edge provides the feeding area, so linear scrapes provide more feeding habitat than round scrapes. Shallow slopes down to a depth of about 45 cm below the early spring water table should ensure good feeding conditions throughout the season. Avoid creating tall bunds as it is important to maintain an open vista. A simple scrape can be excavated, or one can be designed by removing a section of field drain and using a exit pipe to control the outflow level (see Figure 7.2).

Alternatively, a shallow profile can be created along ditch banks or in sections along a ditch by recreating the slope on one or both banks to less than 45°.

Cross-section view

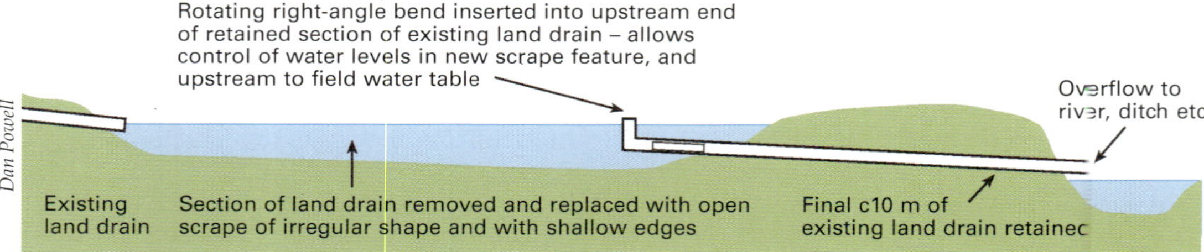

Dan Powell

Plan view

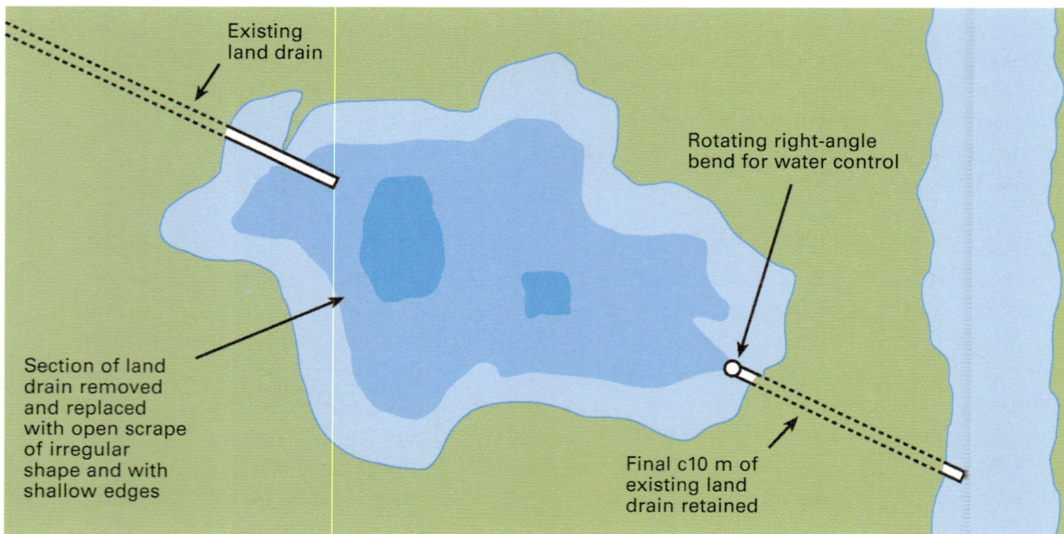

Figure 7.2 Diagram of a drain-fed scrape.

Management of arable land and dry grasslands for lapwings and stone-curlews

Where lapwings and stone-curlews nest in arable situations, a mixed farming system, with grazed pastures and spring-sown arable crops is required. Where either of these features are likely to be lost, nesting and feeding habitat can be provided by creating a summer fallow plot. If possible, the plot should be located in fields where nesting birds have been recorded in the past. Without historical records, they should be sited within 2 km of existing birds in open fields larger than 5 ha (or larger than 10 ha if fields bordered by a wood or tall hedge). If they can be sited next to grazed pasture, then this provides an alternative foraging area for the birds. Stone-curlew plots should not be created within 1 km of major A-roads or motorways, because of disturbance by traffic.

The plots should be at least 2 ha in size, with the shortest dimension no less than 100 m. They should be cultivated annually in February or early March to create a rough tilled surface that breaks up the image of a sitting bird, but allows it to see any approaching predators easily (see Figure 7.3). The plot should remain undisturbed until the end of July, or end of September in the case of nesting stone-curlews, as they can rear two broods in a year. If the regeneration is tall and dense in the early spring and no nesting birds are present, then it would be beneficial to spray or re-cultivate the plot to open it up. It may be advisable to spray before cultivating the plot in subsequent years. Fallow plots can currently be funded by some agri-environment schemes or created on set-aside after receiving a derogation to destroy the green cover.

a) The ideal surface of a lapwing plot.

b) Too rough – newly ploughed land may be too rough unless it has time to weather down by rain or frost before birds arrive.

c) Too flat – land that is rolled or resembles a fine seedbed will generally not be used until vegetation provides some cover for sat birds.

Figure 7.3
Diagram of the ideal surface of a lapwing plot.

Further reading

Benstead P, Drake M, Jose P, Mountford O, Newbold C and Treweek J (1997) *The wet grassland guide: managing floodplain and coastal wet grasslands for wildlife.* The RSPB, Sandy.

Peel S (2001) Guidelines for the reversion of arable land. *Enact* 9, No 4.

Winspear R and Davies G (2005) *A management guide to birds of lowland farmland.* The RSPB, Sandy.

8 Butterflies and moths

8.1 Introduction

The status of butterflies and moths (Lepidoptera) on farmland is of wide interest, not only due to their intrinsic value but because they are increasingly regarded as important biodiversity indicators, both for their rapid and sensitive responses to habitat changes and as representatives of a broad range of wildlife, especially other insects.

The vital importance of lowland farmland to butterflies is emphasised by the fact that it provides breeding habitat for more than 90% (51 out of 55) of resident lowland species. Of the remaining four, the wood white is associated with abandoned farmland at some of its few remaining sites. In addition, the three regular immigrants, clouded yellow, red admiral and painted lady breed commonly on farmland. There are approximately 2,500 species of moth found in Britain, many of which occur on farmland, including a wide range of scarce, threatened and declining species.

For butterflies, the richest and most important farmland habitats are agriculturally unimproved pastures, especially calcareous grasslands, which provide breeding habitat for nearly 90% of species (48 of the 55). Twenty of these have a substantial proportion of their UK population breeding on calcareous grassland, whilst four species, the Lulworth skipper, silver-spotted skipper, chalkhill blue and adonis blue breed exclusively within this habitat.

Other regionally important semi-natural grassland habitats include wet grasslands for orange-tip, green-veined white, small pearl-bordered fritillary and marsh fritillary, and bracken-dominated lower hills, for several threatened fritillaries including the pearl-bordered and high brown. Other rough grazing land of significance to butterflies includes sheltered moorland combes on Exmoor, which are a national stronghold for the rare heath fritillary. All these semi-natural farmland habitats also support a wide diversity of moths.

Arable land and improved grassland supports far fewer species. Only two butterflies (both pests locally) breed widely on cropped land – the large white and small white. However, uncultivated field margins and set-aside can be of considerable value, with at least 32 butterfly species occurring and around 24 species suspected of breeding. Thick, unkempt hedgerows represent perhaps the most important field boundary habitat, especially for gatekeeper, speckled wood, holly blue and the rare brown hairstreak, along with several scarce moths, such as the sloe carpet. Waste ground around farmhouses provide further habitat, especially for nettle-feeders such as the comma and small tortoiseshell. Over 30 species of moths have been recorded utilising nettle as a food plant.

8.2 Populations and distribution

There have been huge declines in farmland butterflies in recent history, with the declines accelerating since the Second World War. At least 15 species have declined in range by more than 25%, four by more than 50%, whilst two species have become extinct. A governmental butterfly biodiversity indicator has recently been compiled for farmland, which shows a drop in the overall abundance of butterflies by about 20% over the last 20 years. In addition to this the farmland environment has seen a drop in the abundance in moths by 46% over the last 25 years (Rothamsted Research, unpublished data).

The declines in butterflies have mainly been in specialist species of semi-natural farmland and a number of more widespread generalist species, such as the peacock, speckled wood, holly blue and Essex skipper, have expanded their ranges, in a northerly/north-westerly direction, thought to be primarily due to climate change.

Factors affecting populations on lowland farmland

The declines in specialist species correspond with losses of semi-natural farmland habitats through agricultural intensification. Subtle changes in habitat quality (the structure, composition and suitability of vegetation) caused by changing management practices have been equally important. This is because most specialists have annual life cycles, and require precise habitat conditions to be present each year. Factors affecting habitat quality include (1) changing grazing practices, such as the abandonment of grazing on marginal land, and the intensification of grazing, especially in upland areas, and (2) the increased use of fertilisers, which has led to a small number of vigorous plant species doing well at the expense of many other larval food plants.

The main causes of decline across intensive farmland has been the loss of hedgerows and associated features. Other damaging farming practices have included:

- the cultivation of former field margins
- annual flailing of hedges
- the widespread use of pesticides and other agro-chemicals and
- increased cutting frequencies and grazing intensities on grasslands.

8.3 Habitat requirements

Butterflies and moths can be conveniently divided into two species types:

- habitat specialists – typically low-mobility species that are chiefly restricted to semi-natural habitats
- habitat generalists – species with relatively high mobility, which occur throughout the landscape in a range of habitat types, including linear features.

For species to persist it is important to meet the requirements of all phases of the life cycle, especially the adults, which undertake the broadest range of activities. In butterflies, basic habitat requirements common to all species are breeding (egg-laying), feeding, roosting, basking, and mate-location habitat located in sunny, sheltered situations for adults; shelter and feeding habitat for larvae and

Tom Brereton

Plate 8.1
A typical good butterfly and moth grassland habitat – containing patches of bare ground, scrub, and an uneven sward structure of coarse tussocky and short herb-rich patches, containing plentiful nectar sources and larval foodplants.

development habitat for the egg and pupal stages.

For specialist species, breeding habitat is a limiting factor, with all species studied shown to have very specific requirements in terms of foodplant species, growth form, sward structure and topography. This high degree of habitat selectivity tends to limit them to discrete (often high density) populations in specific patches of semi-natural farmland habitat. Generalist species tend to have more catholic tastes, hence breeding vegetation is more widely available across the farmed landscape, though it is often dispersed at low density or concentrated along field boundaries of intensively farmed crops and pastures.

Adult butterflies and moths may use a range of differing sward structures and

Table 8.1 Habitat requirements of UK BAP Priority butterfly and moth species on farmland.

Species	Distribution on farmland	Habitat requirements
Adonis blue	Unimproved calcareous grassland in southern England	Horseshoe vetch growing on south-facing slopes in broken turf chiefly 0–4 cm tall
Marsh fritillary	Unimproved (1) wet or (2) calcareous grassland in western Britain	Devil's-bit scabious and/or small scabious growing either (1) amongst 8–25 cm tall tussocky damp grass or (2) in 5–15 cm tall calcareous grassland (usually on west- or south-facing slopes)
Heath fritillary	Sheltered combes on Exmoor	Sunny, sheltered heathland combes containing bilberry and common cow-wheat, often with bramble nectar nearby
High brown fritillary	Bracken-dominated lower hill land in western England and Wales	Dog-violets growing in sunny situations (in June–August) through flattened beds of bracken litter on south-facing slopes, with plentiful nectar sources nearby
Pearl-bordered fritillary	Bracken-dominated lower hill land in western and northern Britain	Dog-violets growing in sunny situations (in May–June) through flattened beds of bracken litter on south-facing slopes, with plentiful nectar sources nearby
Silver-spotted skipper	Unimproved calcareous grassland in southern England	Close-cropped grasslands containing small tufts (1–5 cm tall) of sheep's-fescue that grow in warm hollows and amongst bare ground patches, with plentiful nectar sources nearby
Sloe carpet*	Hedgerows and scrub in south-east England	Overgrown blackthorn in hedgerows or as scattered scrub on grasslands in a sunny situation
Barberry carpet	Hedgerows in southern and eastern England	Barberry bushes in hedgerows and other situations. The highest populations occur where the barberry is lightly trimmed rather than being heavily cut or left uncut
Barred tooth-striped	Scrub, usually on calcareous soils throughout England	Usually associated with mature wild privet scrub in a sunny situation
Black-veined moth	Calcareous grassland in East Kent	Extensive marjoram in rank turf. The larvae require dead grass stems to be left throughout the winter and spring
Buttoned snout	Hedgerows in south-east England and south Wales	Hop in hedgerows
Chalk carpet	Calcareous grassland throughout England and Wales	Bird's-foot-trefoil and other trefoils and clovers on calcareous grassland with frequent bare ground patches
Four-spotted	Field edges and other marginal land in southern and eastern England	Field bindweed, particularly at field edges, on verges and along ditches. Bindweed growing in light vegetation is preferred
Heart moth	Hedgerow and parkland trees in the southern half of England	Ancient oak trees growing in an open situation such as in hedgerows, parkland and permanent pasture
Marsh mallow moth	River and ditch banks on coastal grazing marshes in Kent and East Sussex	Marsh mallow along rivers and ditches with some salinity. The food plant needs to be protected from grazing, especially during the summer months
Netted carpet	Grazed woodland in the Lake District	Touch-me-not balsam in damp woodlands. Winter cattle grazing is beneficial in creating the bare ground that the food plant requires but summer grazing results in loss of the food plant
Pale shining brown	Field edges, hedgerows and scrubby calcareous grassland in southern and eastern England	Requirements not currently fully understood.
Straw belle	Calcareous grassland on the North Downs	The larvae require patches of bare ground over which they bask in the spring. Adults require longer turf
Striped lychnis	Calcareous grassland and verges in central southern England	Dark mullein on sparsely vegetated calcareous grassland

*Candidate BAP Priority Species

Dan Hoare

Plate 8.2
Barberry bushes, a plant persecuted in the past, can support the endangered barberry carpet moth.

vegetation features for other behavioural activities. A number of habitat specialist butterfly species such as the chalkhill blue, dingy skipper, grizzled skipper, silver-studded blue and moths such as the straw belle, which require short vegetation for egg-laying, utilise taller vegetation such as ungrazed seed heads or grass tussocks for roosting. Many species spend substantial amounts of time feeding on nectar, and the presence of large quantities of plants in flower is important for some species and may affect local abundance.

Bare ground is required by a number of species, through providing both warmth and camouflage. Bare ground is used for basking and shelter, whilst a number of specialist species preferentially lay their eggs on food plants growing on bare ground. Aspect and slope is important for a number of specialist species, with for example the adonis blue, pearl-bordered fritillary and straw belle restricted to warm south-facing slopes.

Hedgerows and patches of scrub can be important for adult butterflies by providing shelter, and roosting and mate-location habitat. Ivy and sallow blossom are invaluable nectar sources at a time of year when other nectar sources are scarce.

It is important to take into account the needs of the immature stages, as their requirements may be quite different to the adult stage. For example, the grizzled skipper prefers food plants growing amongst short vegetation and over bare ground. However, later stage larvae frequently move into much ranker vegetation to feed, which may be crucial for successful development.

For low mobility habitat specialist species, the differing resources required by the adult and immature stages need to be in close proximity usually within a discrete habitat patch.

8.4 Management advice

Semi-natural grassland

In general terms, the objective of habitat management for butterflies is to create heterogeneity – sites that contain a herb-rich and varied sward structure through the growing season, plentiful nectar sources, frequent patches of bare ground, and stands of both scattered and dense scrub should support a rich fauna.

Stock grazing is the main mechanism through which UK BAP Priority and other habitat specialist butterflies and moths can be conserved on semi-natural grassland, with a degree of grazing beneficial for practically all species. A wide range of stock grazing regimes can be deployed successfully. However, it is important to highlight that no single grazing regime can be relied on to maintain suitable conditions year in year out, as habitat condition is determined by other factors such as annual weather conditions and rabbit densities. Success is to a large degree determined by careful planning and timing of management, focused on creating and maintaining the right habitat condition, with fine-tuning as required (eg to prevent over- or undergrazing).

On large sites (more than 100 ha) year-round cattle grazing at relatively high stocking densities (more than one livestock unit per hectare, LU/ha), has been shown to benefit a wide range of species with differing requirements. Grazing regimes with mixed stock types can also be highly beneficial (eg winter cattle, summer sheep), whilst periodic heavy winter grazing may be of value in helping to maintain high herb densities in the long term.

No individual stock breeds can be singled out as particularly beneficial, though hardy cattle breeds known to create good habitat include Dexter, Galloway, Belted Galloway, North Devon and Red Poll cattle, whilst Hebridean, Wiltshire Horn and Herdwick sheep can play a vital role in controlling bramble and other scrub.

In practise, conserving populations of habitat specialists involves some tailoring of management to the specific needs of individual species especially in relation to sward structure and the location of larval food plants. It is important to determine the key species present at each site, as species may have very different requirements. For example on calcareous grasslands, although many species require short turf for breeding, the Duke of Burgundy (a rapidly declining UK BAP Species of Conservation Concern) requires rank, often scrubby swards containing abundant cowslips or primroses and the black-veined moth (a UK BAP Priority species) requires rank, or recently abandoned, grassland with abundant marjoram. For other species, such as the lunar yellow underwing moth, fine-leaved grass tussocks are important. In cases where species with conflicting requirements co-occur, carefully targeting of management is required and it may be beneficial to seek specialist advice.

As part of management planning, assessment is required of the topography (eg soil conditions, slope), natural processes (eg erosion, rabbit grazing) and land management practices that have created and maintained suitable habitat conditions in the past, especially before making any management changes. For example, an abandoned grassland site may have considerable interest, due to the presence of a stable rabbit population, and stock grazing may not be required in the short-term to maintain the interest. If the objective is to combine wildlife conservation with farming by restoring agricultural use, control of the rabbit population will be required. Failure to do so, could lead to overgrazing and loss of the butterfly and moth interest. For sites where sheep grazing is being introduced to replace moderate to heavy rabbit grazing, consideration should be given as to how sufficient bare ground will be created as this is unlikely to be achieved by sheep grazing alone (unless the slope is very steep). In southern England, rabbit grazing is likely to be a feature at every single calcareous grassland site. For some specialist species, including dark green fritillary, silver-spotted skipper, Duke of Burgundy and small blue, nationally important populations can be maintained solely by rabbit grazing, though excessive overgrazing by rabbits can lead to declines of the same species. For management prescriptions, stocking levels must be set in relation to the level of rabbit grazing if they are to have any meaning. In the case of the adonis blue, stocking levels of less than 0.1 LU/ha are sufficient at heavily rabbit grazed sites, whilst at lightly rabbit grazed sites typical stocking levels at good sites in the region of 0.8 LU/ha can work well.

Rabbit and stock grazing combinations work extremely well at many sites, particularly winter stock grazing regimes; with stock playing a vital role in removing litter and grass growth at the end of the growing season, and patchy rabbit grazing creating bare ground and a variable turf through the spring and summer.

Scrub is an important component of good butterfly and moth habitat on grassland, but requires regular management to prevent loss of grassland. As part of stock grazing restoration, scrub clearance may be beneficial in improving habitat quality and increasing site carrying capacity for the key species present. In addition to clearance, the maintenance and successional management of scrub on rotation can be vital to a range of species such as the dark green fritillary, Duke of

Burgundy, high brown fritillary and pearl-bordered fritillary. Gorse cutting on a 2–6 year rotation is an example of a regime benefiting both dark green and pearl-bordered fritillaries. Care should be taken however, as some species, such as the sloe carpet favour mature blackthorn scrub. Others, such as the dingy mocha, require a plentiful supply of small, isolated sallow bushes growing in sunny situations, for breeding. Rotational bracken management is an important tool to maintain suitable habitat conditions for the dark green fritillary, pearl-bordered fritillary and high brown fritillary. Cutting bracken in strips (less than 50% per annum) outside the growing season on a 2–5 year rotation has worked well for these species at some sites.

Periodic winter burning (to control scrub and rejuvenate bilberry) in combination with grazing is an essential component of management for the heath fritillary in moorland combe habitats on Exmoor. In the absence of grazing, burning can also be used to manage marsh fritillary wet grassland habitats, though only part of the site should be burned in any one year and it should only be carried out on sites with a history of burning.

Grass cutting should be considered as an alternative way of maintaining grassland habitat at sites where grazing cannot be restored for practical reasons (eg urban fringe sites and in regions with few stock animals). Species that have benefited from annual mowing (especially autumn flail mowing at 5–10 cm blade height) include chalkhill blue, dark green fritillary, dingy skipper, Duke of Burgundy (in combination with scrub management), grizzled skipper, heath fritillary and marsh fritillary.

Arable land and improved grassland

A number of measures can be undertaken to encourage butterflies and moths on intensive farmland, including creating new habitats such as grassy field margins and rough field corners, better hedgerow management, tree planting and reducing agro-chemical inputs, including spray drift, particularly around field edges.

Management effort should focus on hedgerows and cereal field margins, as these are amongst the most important habitats for butterflies and moths and financial incentives are available under agri-environment schemes for improved management.

Hedges can provide valuable breeding areas, especially if they contain standard trees, the hedge verge is still intact and woodland herbs are in the hedge bottom and banks. Mixed hedges are best – for example, those with blackthorn can support the rare brown hairstreak and sloe carpet, while those with buckthorn or alder buckthorn suit the brimstone butterfly. Over 100 species of moth are known to utilise blackthorn as a host plant and over 25 species can utilise the buckthorns. A wide range of other hedgerow plants can support equally impressive assemblages of species.

Plants in hedge verges can also provide food for larvae; for example grasses support gatekeepers and ringlets, the orange-tip uses garlic mustard, the comma, peacock, small tortoiseshell and red admiral use nettles, whilst a wide variety of low-growing plants are used by other species. An adjacent supply of tall herb nectar sources such as creeping thistle and fleabane is important for hedge breeding species such as the brown hairstreak. The larval stage of nearly 200 species of moth

Plate 8.3 Fleabane is important for hedge breeding species such as the brown hairstreak.

Peter Creed

Tom Brereton

Plate 8.4 Common blue – a butterfly, which benefits from uncropped field margins, sown with legumes and nectar plants.

are associated with seeds and fruit, and it is important that there is a plentiful supply for these species to complete their life cycle. Hedges and verges also provide suitable conditions for overwintering, though some species need taller vegetation and require uncut areas. The presence of mature trees can attract canopy-dwelling species – with elms providing breeding habitat for white-letter hairstreak and white-spotted pinion (a UK BAP Priority Species), and oaks for purple hairstreak. Ancient oaks in hedgerows or a parkland setting may support rare species, such as the heart moth. Fungus infected trees and fallen branches also have a small associated moth fauna, with just over 20 species linked to the fungi and many of these could be found on farmland.

Hedges should be cut to maintain a variety of shapes and sizes across the farm and on rotation so that each section is cut, for example, every 2–5 years. Cutting should take place in January or February when most insects are in their dormant phase. Annual cutting of all hedges on the farm could be very damaging especially if it is done over a short time scale.

There are a number of options open to enable farmers to create grassy margins around cereal fields that have potential to be highly attractive to butterflies and moths. Margins should be left to regenerate naturally if colonisation by a variety of native plant species is likely to be rapid (eg through good semi-natural habitats being present nearby) or alternatively sown with native, locally sourced, grasses and wild flowers that contain both annual and perennial wild flowers. Crucifers, legumes, Asteraceae and fine-leaved grasses are particularly valuable for a range of common grassland butterflies.

For 2 m and 6 m margins to be of interest to butterflies and moths, they need to contain structural and species diversity (as described for semi-natural grassland). Margins that comprise dense, monocultures of coarse grasses may do more harm than good, if they replace more diverse vegetation between the hedge and the crop. Not all margins should be cut every year to enable butterflies and moths to breed and complete their life cycles, with a proportion cut on 2–5 year rotations in the autumn to prevent scrub and dominance by rank grasses. Conservation headlands (with reduced or no spraying) can be beneficial, as they will reduce herbicide and pesticide penetration into hedge bases and can provide nectar sources through the summer.

Numbers of butterflies and moths can build up rapidly if large quantities of favoured nectar sources such as black knapweed, common valerian, field scabious, fleabane, marjoram, teasel, hemp-agrimony, viper's bugloss and bird's-foot-trefoil are present, eg by sowing a pollen and nectar mix. Cutting should occur unevenly across the farm to create a mosaic of vegetation heights and to allow re-colonisation of the less mobile invertebrate species from other margins.

Conserving farmyard butterflies and moths can even start from the doorstep. Around farmyards, patches of nettles in sunny positions should be retained and cutting about a third of them in mid-July will create young growth favoured by the summer brood of small tortoiseshells.

Further reading

Asher J, Warren M, Fox R, Harding P, Jeffcoate G, Jeffcoate S (2001) *The Millennium atlas of butterflies in Britain and Ireland*. Oxford University Press, Oxford.

Brereton T (2004) Farming and butterflies. *The Biologist* 51, 32–36.

Butterflies Under Threat Team (BUTT) (1986) *The management of chalk downland for butterflies.* Nature Conservancy Council, Peterborough, UK

Conrad K F, Perry J N, Woiwod I P and Alexander C J (2006) Large-scale temporal changes in spatial pattern during declines of abundance and occupancy in a common moth. *Journal of Insect Conservation*, 10, 53–64.

Dover J W (1996) Factors affecting the distribution of butterflies on arable farmland. *Journal of Applied Ecology*, 33, 723–734.

Feber R E, Smith H and Macdonald D W (1996) The effects of management of uncropped edges of arable fields on butterfly abundance. *Journal of Applied Ecology*, 33, 1191–1205.

Fox R, Asher J, Brereton T, Roy D and Warren M (2006) *The state of butterflies in Britain and Ireland.* Pisces Publications, Newbury, Berkshire.

Fox R, Conrad K F, Parsons M S, Warren M S and Woiwod I P (2006) *The state of Britain's larger moths.* Butterfly Conservation and Rothamsted Research, Wareham.

Parsons M S, Fox R, Conrad K F, Woiwod I P and Warren M S (2005) British moths: throwing light on a new conservation challenge. *British Wildlife*, 16(6), 386–394.

Pywell R F, Warman E A, Sparks T H, Greatorex-Davis J N, Walker K J, Meek W R, Carvell C, Petit S and Firbank L G (2004) Assessing habitat quality for butterflies on intensively managed farmland. *Biological Conservation*, 118, 313–325.

Young M (1997) *The natural history of moths.* Poyser Natural History, London.

BAP Priority Species Factsheets – available from Butterfly Conservation at http://www.butterfly-conservation.org/conservation/defrafactsheets/index

9 Grasshoppers and bush-crickets

9.1 Introduction

Grasshoppers and bush-crickets, collectively known as the Orthoptera, are a critical invertebrate prey group for a number of declining farmland birds, including the cirl bunting and yellowhammer. During the breeding season, these species require invertebrate prey to feed their chicks. Whilst spiders and caterpillars are important during the early part of the breeding season, Orthoptera become one of the main prey items from July onwards.

Unfortunately, there are no data describing long-term population trends of grasshoppers and bush-crickets on UK farmland, but they are likely to have declined in line with other insect groups such as butterflies and moths as a consequence of changes in farming. Although agri-environment schemes target the general enhancement of farmland biodiversity and not specifically Orthoptera, they do have the potential to significantly increase both the area and quality of habitats for grasshoppers and bush-crickets.

9.2 Populations and distributions

Twenty-seven species of native Orthoptera have been recorded breeding in the UK. None are strongly associated with farmland, but a number of the more common species have been recorded on habitats associated with farmland. The meadow grasshopper is probably the most common and widespread species. There are areas where it appears to be absent, including parts of the east coast, where the lesser marsh grasshopper is the most common species and parts of the midland plain, where the common green grasshopper predominates. Other common species of Orthoptera that have been recorded in farmland habitats include the field grasshopper, dark bush-cricket and speckled bush-cricket. The distributions of these species are concentrated in the southern part of the UK. The long-winged cone-head and Roesel's bush-cricket are rapidly expanding their ranges from the far south and east of mainland Britain and as a result may become more common on farmland habitats. Other species recorded on farmland include the great green bush-

Peter Creed

Plate 9.1 Long-winged cone-head is rapidly expanding in range.

cricket, which is confined to the southern half of England and tends to be more common in coastal areas, common ground-hopper, which is widely distributed throughout the UK, and slender ground-hopper, which is widely distributed within southern and central England.

Factors affecting populations

Short-term studies on Orthoptera suggest that populations may have declined as a consequence of increased insecticide use, the improvement of pastures through the input of nitrogen, phosphorous and potassium and the loss and isolation of suitable habitat. Intensive grazing regimes will have a negative impact on many Orthoptera species and mowing in July has been shown to have a detrimental effect on the meadow grasshopper, and probably impacts other Orthopteran species similarly.

9.3 Habitat requirements

Many of the UK grasshopper and bush-cricket species that occur on farmland are habitat generalists. They can occur in a range of different habitats and are only absent from a few relatively harsh or intensively managed habitats (eg intensive dairy pastures and arable fields). All UK grasshopper species require grassy swards, but none are associated with any particular grass species or genera. Bush-crickets generally require longer, rougher unmanaged grassland or scrubby areas. All species benefit from a

Table 9.1 Habitat requirements of common Orthoptera species on farmland.

Species	Habitat preferences
Meadow grasshopper	Found in variety of grassland habitats, but most numerous in damp meadows and in dry coarse, rough grassland. High densities (> 3 individuals per m^2) have been recorded in arable margins and non-rotational set-aside. Tends to be scarce on short, improved pastures.
Lesser marsh grasshopper	Despite preferring damp grasslands, it has been found in dry grassland habitats. Recorded on set-aside and other non-intensive farmed habitats. In eastern counties of England it can be the most abundant species of Orthoptera at a location. Colonisation of farmed habitats more likely as range expands.
Common green grasshopper	Prefers coarse long grass in moist situations, which is not heavily grazed or mown. In particular, this species favours old, unimproved pastures. Where the soil is damp, this species can tolerate shorter swards.
Field grasshopper	Found in a variety of grassland habitats. Prefers dry, sunny situations with a short sward and patches of exposed soil. Scarce in wet habitats or where the sward is too tall and dense. Recorded on arable margins and agri-environment pastures with suitable swards.
Dark bush-cricket	Most common in scrub and is particularly associated with bramble. Also found in coarse herbage along hedgerows, overgrown ditches and nettle-beds. Recorded most frequently in arable margins, particularly those that are overgrown.
Speckled bush-cricket	Frequents rough herbage, scrub and hedgerows. Found in arable margins and non-rotational set-aside.
Long-winged cone-head	Found in coarse unmanaged vegetation and in long grass in warm, sunny locations. Found in high densities on some non-rotational set-aside and arable margins. Colonisation of farmed habitats more likely as range expands.
Roesel's bush-cricket	Usually found in coarse, unmanaged vegetation in warm and sunny locations. Recorded on set-aside and arable margins. Colonisation of farmed habitats more likely as range expands.
Great green bush-cricket	Associated with warm sunny locations containing rough unmanaged herbage, usually with brambles and unkempt scrub. Thin turf or bare ground essential for egg laying. Has been recorded in arable margins, non-rotational set-aside and occasionally in cultivated cropped habitats.
Common ground-hopper and slender ground-hopper	Common ground-hopper requires bare ground and short vegetation. It is able to tolerate both wet and dry locations. Slender ground-hopper requires similar habitat conditions, but is restricted to damp unshaded locations. These two species have been recorded in arable margins, extensively grazed pasture and on a limited number of set-aside fields.

warm, sunny, sheltered location. In the UK, the presence of any one species will be greatly determined by the geographical location of a site in combination with the coverage and quality of the local habitat. In general, there is a tendency for the potential number of species of grasshopper and bush-cricket in a location to decline with increases in latitude. Table 9.1 summarises broad habitat preferences for a selection of common UK Orthoptera that are most likely to occur on farmed habitats.

9.4 Management advice

In general, management should aim to achieve a mosaic of different sward heights suitable for the grasshopper and bush-cricket species present. The most important point is that cutting of grasslands and arable margins should be left until as late as possible in the season, preferably not before early September. This allows enough time for individuals to mature, mate and lay eggs. Orthoptera may also benefit if the sward is cut early in the season, before mid-May. This, however, may impact on other farmland flora and fauna, such as ground-nesting birds and certain butterfly and moth species. Cutting before the end of March will protect nesting birds. Suitable habitat patches can be small, but should preferably be greater than 0.5 ha in area. If possible, habitat patches should be connected to each other using linear corridors, which will allow animals to move between areas. If this is not possible, isolated habitat patches should be located in close proximity to each other (closer the better, but preferably less than 100 m), because it will help animals move between suitable habitat patches. In any habitat, most Orthopteran species benefit from the presence of small patches of bare ground created by grazing animals, moles or the yellow meadow ant because such areas are suitable for basking and egg laying. Finally, most grasshopper and bush-cricket species will favour sites that face south and east. If possible, this should be considered when selecting new areas for habitat creation.

The intensity of management needed will differ on a site-by-site basis dependent on the species of grasshopper and bush-cricket present, as well as factors such as soil fertility and farming practice. Swards on fertile soils, for example, are likely to require a more intensive management regime (eg higher stocking density) than those on light, relatively infertile soils. On organic farms some of the management advice, in particular the period when swards should be cut, might have to be offset by the demands of controlling pernicious weed species, such as thistle. Conventional farming methods, however,

Greg Hitchcock/wildaboutkent.com

Plate 9.2 Meadow grasshopper

should be able to accommodate many of the recommendations with relative ease.

An orthoptera survey should be undertaken to determine the management that will conserve species diversity. If the objective is to increase overall abundance of grasshoppers (eg for bird food) then management can be targeted at the most common species present. For the vast majority of sites, the meadow grasshopper is likely to be the most common species, as well as the species of grasshopper that most birds feed on. Sward structure, rather than botanical diversity, will determine the abundance of this species and the diversity of other orthoptera. Young nymphs develop in short swards (< 15 cm) and as they mature they move into taller swards (10–25 cm), probably because these the microclimate in these swards is cooler. Taller swards also provide cover from inclement weather and predators. Adults prefer swards between 30 and 50 cm, but may prefer shorter swards where rye-grass or purple moor-grass are dominant. Therefore, management should aim to create swards where ranges of short and long swards are adjacent to each other. This patchwork, which can be created through suitable grazing or cutting regimes, will also provide areas where foraging birds can access prey items within the sward. If swards are sown for grasshoppers, rye-grass species should be avoided and a mixture of bents, fescues and Yorkshire-fog or related species should be included. A small amount of cock's-foot in the sward might be beneficial, but high densities are likely to have a negative effect because of the resulting dense, tussocky sward. Again, cutting should be delayed until as late as possible and there is some circumstantial evidence that grasshoppers benefit if the cutting height is raised above 15 cm.

In some geographical locations the most abundant species might be lesser marsh grasshopper (eastern England), common green grasshopper (midland plain, the north and at higher altitudes) or the field grasshopper. What little evidence there is on habitat preferences suggests that the first two also prefer tall rather than short swards, whereas the field grasshopper prefers a short more open sward, with patches of bare ground. Although they are unlikely to be found on most farmed habitats in the UK, the striped-winged and mottled grasshoppers also prefer short, open turfs with bare ground. The striped-winged grasshopper is most likely to be encountered along the length of the North and South Downs and is widespread in the chalk grasslands of Wiltshire, Berkshire, Hampshire and Purbeck Hill area in Dorset. The mottled grasshopper is widespread usually occurring on free-draining soils on sand, gravels, chalk and limestone.

Table 9.1 illustrates that many of the bush-cricket species, such the great green, Roesel's, speckled and dark bush-crickets as well as the long-winged cone-head, are associated with tall, coarse, unmanaged grasslands. These tend to contain relatively high abundances of forb and scrub species, such as thistles, nettles and bramble (important for dark bush-crickets). This can be achieved in both arable margins and pasture habitats by decreasing the frequency and intensity of cutting and grazing. The conservation value of these unmanaged areas will be enhanced if they are placed in sheltered and sunny locations. Furthermore, these areas of unmanaged grassland should be located adjacent to hedgerows. The interface between pasture or arable margin and the hedge should preferably be untidy. This can be achieved by rarely managing areas within 1–2 m of the hedge. On non-rotational set-aside, up to 2 m next to the hedge can remain uncut without any specific exemption. This will greatly enhance the habitat for bush-crickets.

Arable land

On arable land, 6 m agri-environment grass margins have been shown to greatly benefit grasshoppers, although in some locations 6 m margins contain no or very few grasshoppers. To maximise the conservation value, margins should be managed to provide the widest range of habitats utilised by Orthoptera. For example, the edge next to the hedge should be cut less frequently (every three years), and the rest of the margin should be cut annually or every other year (in early September) to ensure a grassy sward is maintained. If possible, sections of margins within the same field should be cut on a rotational basis so that mixtures of sward height and age occur in close proximity to each other. If possible, follow the sward composition recommendations above (ie avoid rye-grass and high abundances of cock's-foot). Meadow grasshoppers, however, will not benefit if the whole margin becomes too scrubby or dominated by non-grass species, such as nettle, bracken and bramble. Management should therefore aim to keep most of the margin free of these plants. Arable margins of 2 m widths tend to suffer encroachment to a greater extent than 6 m margins and as a consequence tend to be dominated by non-grass species. On 2 m arable margins cutting might have to be conducted annually to maintain a grassy sward. Insecticide drift might impact populations of grasshoppers on arable margins therefore conservation headlands or buffer strips are likely to be of benefit.

If managed correctly, fixed set-aside has the potential to greatly increase the abundance (and diversity) of grasshoppers at any site. Under current rules, 25% of each set-aside area can be left uncut for up to three years without any specific exemption. This will greatly benefit the meadow grasshopper (and other Orthoptera species) provided that the set-aside does not become too overgrown or dominated by non-grass species. If possible, areas of set-aside should be connected by arable margins because animals will move down the length of the margin to other potentially suitable areas. Populations of grasshoppers on arable margins might also benefit if they are connected to extensively managed pastures (eg managed under agri-environment schemes), which tend to provide the short swards suitable for egg and nymphal development.

Grassland

In the majority of agricultural grassland habitats grasshoppers will benefit from less intensive management. On intensive dairy pastures, avoiding inorganic fertiliser applications on grass margins will be beneficial. The potential benefit of this will be greatly enhanced if the margins are not cut and the frequency and intensity of grazing is reduced. On extensively managed agri-environment grazed pastures, sward heights are frequently too short to support adult grasshoppers. A slight reduction in grazing intensity might therefore be beneficial. Through rotational grazing it should be possible to create fields that have patches of different sward heights, some areas should have swards of 30 cm to 50 cm, others 10 cm to 25 cm, whilst adjacent areas should contain swards less than 15 cm. On a number of agri-environment pastures in south Devon, small areas of sparse stunted bracken growth appear to benefit grasshoppers, probably as a consequence of the reduced grazing pressure in and around the bracken patches. Bracken is currently regarded as an injurious weed on grasslands, but a small amount of bracken will benefit Orthoptera, as well as other grassland invertebrate species. Managements should therefore aim to maintain or perhaps introduce these small-scattered patches of sparse bracken growth. Large solid patches of bracken, however, should be avoided.

Further reading

Bioimages, the virtual field guide (UK): www.bioimages.org.uk/HTML/T365.HTM

Brown V K (1990) *Grasshoppers*. The Richmond Publishing Co. Ltd., Slough, UK.

Clark E J (1948) Studies in the ecology of British grasshoppers. *The Transactions of the Royal Entomological Society of London*, 99, 173–222.

Gardiner T, Pye M, Field R and Hill J (2002) The influence of sward height and vegetation composition in determining the habitat preferences of three Chorthippus species (Orthoptera: Acrididae) in Chelmsford, Essex, UK. *Journal of Orthoptera Research*, 11, 207–213.

Gardiner T and Hill J (2006) Mortality of Orthoptera caused by mechanised mowing of grassland. *British Journal of Entomology and Natural History*, 19, 38–40.

Haes E C M and Harding P T (1997) *Atlas of grasshoppers, crickets and allied insects in Britain and Ireland*. The Stationery Office, London.

Marshall J A and Haes E C M (1990) *Grasshoppers and allied insects of Great Britain and Ireland*. Harley Books, Colchester, UK.

Richards O W and Waloff N (1954) Studies on the biology and population dynamics of British grasshoppers. *Anti-Locust Bulletin*, 17, 1–182.

van Wingerden W K R E, Musters J C M, Kleukers R M J C, Bongers W and van Biezen J B (1991) The influence of cattle grazing intensity on grasshopper abundance (Orthoptera: Acrididae). *Proceedings Experiment and Applied Entomology*, N.E.V., Amsterdam, 2, 28–34.

van Wingerden W K R E, van Kreveld A R and Bongers W (1992) Analysis of species composition and abundances of grasshoppers (Orth., Acrididae) in natural and fertilized grasslands. *Journal of Applied Entomology*, 113, 138–152.

10 Dragonflies and other aquatic insects

10.1 Introduction

Populations of dragonflies and other aquatic insects on farmland are threatened by the loss of wetland habitats and pollution. All wetland habitats, however small, can be managed for aquatic invertebrates. Being predators, dragonflies are near the top of the wetland food chain and can indicate the health of ponds and watercourses for wildlife. Many smaller insects, such as non-biting midges, also emerge from water in huge numbers, providing food for birds and other animals.

Adult dragonflies and damselflies are often conspicuous and brightly coloured. Dragonflies are relatively large and fast flying, and hold their wings out at right angles to the body when at rest. Damselflies are generally smaller, weaker and hold their wings together or partly open when at rest.

This section focuses on dragonflies and damselflies, as a popular, relatively easily identified and well-known group. However, their varying preferences as a group means that, by managing wetlands for them, many other aquatic insects will also benefit.

10.2 Populations and distributions

There are 42 dragonfly and damselfly species breeding regularly in the UK, but like other insects more species can be found in the warmer south and west. However, their distribution is often highly localised, due to the isolation of their habitats or very specific habitat requirements. A farm pond in southern England should be capable of hosting over 10 'generalist' breeding species, while a ditch on a sympathetically-managed grazing marsh with good water quality can have over 15, some of which are nationally scarce. Some of the best sites are on heathland, where the acidic water limits the populations of predatory fish and over 20 species may be found.

Three breeding species were lost from the UK during 1953–1965. Climate change has led to dramatic colonisations and

David Smallshire

Plate 10.1 Broad-bodied chaser

northward spread by southern species (including some from the Continent). However, one northern species of heathland bogs has probably declined as a result of climate change.

10.3 Habitat requirements

In common with many other insects, dragonflies and damselflies have an aquatic larval stage. Although the adult stage typically lasts only a matter of days, the larvae of most species take one or two years to mature (range four months to five years). During this period, the quality and depth of water and the abundance and variety of aquatic plants and associated animals are paramount. After emerging from water, the adults require shelter nearby where they can hunt their insect prey and roost at night and during bad weather.

In general, dragonflies and damselflies need:

- unpolluted water, generally less than 1 m deep
- abundant submerged native pondweeds
- abundant prey such as insects, water-fleas and tadpoles
- few or no introduced fish and waterfowl
- shallow margins with emergent plants on which larvae emerge
- trees, bushes and other tall vegetation nearby, but mostly not overshading.

10.4 Management advice

Buffer strips next to all watercourses and water bodies

Good water quality is an essential requirement of most aquatic life, and will be affected by any inputs of fertiliser, pesticides or eroded soil. Wide strips of unsprayed perennial vegetation (woodland, grassland or other habitat) will help to protect all forms of watercourse and waterbody. It is beneficial to keep most of the water's edge free of tree cover, especially conifers and particularly on the south bank, to prevent excessive shading and leaf litter, although cover such as broadleaved trees and shrubs within 100 m of the edge is beneficial for many species.

Nutrient enrichment from sewage effluent and agricultural sources gives rise to excessive growth of algae and duckweed; this can cause deoxygenation and eliminate underwater vegetation and the animals (such as dragonflies) which depend on it.

Lakes and ponds

The general principle is to maintain as much stable shallow water with native aquatic vegetation as possible. Shallow margins provide more opportunity for submerged and emergent plants to establish and are less prone to bank erosion than steeply shelved shorelines. Few species can tolerate widely fluctuating water levels, so it is beneficial to avoid water abstraction from the lakes or their sources, where possible. Trampled and bare muddy pond margins are attractive to some specialised aquatic species, including a few dragonflies. However, access for farm animals or humans should be restricted to small areas using fencing that extends into the pond.

Many exotic pondweeds and marginal plants are invasive and may dominate large areas if not controlled. These species should not be introduced and any which appear naturally should be removed before they become established. Cutting or pulling is generally ineffective after plants have become established and any control achieved usually lasts for only one season. Treatment by herbicide may be possible in specific circumstances, but consent is required from the Environment Agency (England and Wales), Scottish Environment Protection Agency (Scotland) or Department of Environment (Northern Ireland) before applying herbicides in or near water. Some native plants, notably reed and reedmace, are invasive and hence inappropriate in smaller waters. The pointed rhizomes of reedmace and some *Carex* sedges may puncture pond liners. The removal of aquatic vegetation should be kept to a minimum, and any vegetation removed should be left close to the bank for a day to allow some of the invertebrates and amphibians to return to the water.

Introduced animals are also damaging to the aquatic environment, particularly introduced fish and waterfowl, which predate invertebrates or the aquatic vegetation that supports them, stir up the substrate and raise water nutrient levels. Smaller waterbodies are more susceptible to these problems.

New lakes or ponds can be created for dragonflies, but it is important to check first that you are not destroying an existing unimproved habitat and that the water source is sufficiently unpolluted. New waters may require planning permission and an abstraction and impounding licence. As a general guide, if the pond can be created using machinery normally available on the farm, and is for nature conservation or agricultural use, it will not require planning permission. However, regulation is complex and the Environment Agency, SEPA or DoE(NI) should be consulted when planning ponds or lakes.

A test dig will help to determine whether the pond is likely to hold water naturally or whether a liner will be needed. Linings can be puddled clay, concrete, Bentonite, pre-formed, plastic (polyethylene or PVC) or butyl rubber. A series of small ponds is better for dragonflies than a single large one. Such ponds can be of different dimensions and subsequently cleared at different times, providing for the widest range of habitats for dragonflies and other species. Plan the margins of new lakes and ponds to have shallow slopes (less than 1 in 3), extensive areas of shallow water (less than 50 cm deep) and a convoluted shoreline. The deepest point should be at least 75 cm (60 cm for a pool of less than 20 m^2) to reduce the risk of completely drying out in the summer. Avoid planting any trees very close to the margin. Ideally, any overhanging vegetation should be on the northern margin and no more than 25% of the southern margins should be shaded.

Natural colonisation by dragonflies is usually rapid – there is no need to introduce them. However, it may be beneficial to introduce native plants, especially underwater pondweeds, ideally from a local source. It is normal for new ponds to experience an algal bloom until the new plant and animal communities have become more balanced. The 'problem' may resolve naturally, as blooms may come and go. A thriving pondweed community will assist by competing for light and nutrients. If problems persist, a poor quality water supply is likely to be the reason. Barley straw in mesh bags submerged just below the water's surface in spring may give some control of algae. As the straw decomposes, chemicals released inhibit algal growth. Use 25–50 g of straw per square metre of water, replacing it when it turns black. Avoid topping up with tap water, as this contains chlorine and more nutrients than rainwater.

Eventually, natural succession causes all waters to become choked with vegetation and eventually to dry out. The need for open water varies with species. Generally, fewer dragonfly species occur as open water disappears, which may be in less than five years in the case of garden ponds; larger and deeper waters, however, may take more than a century. If sediment build up at a pond inlet requires desilting more than once a decade, then it would be worthwhile installing a sediment trap upstream. It is important to leave some ponds at a mature stage (ie with little open water) to benefit those species which depend on them. If you have a number of ponds, try to manage them sequentially over a decade or more, to provide a range of successional stages – clearing all out at once should be avoided. Whatever the size of a site, a general rule would be to clear no more than half the area in any one year, in autumn/winter. When clearing out a pond with steep banks, consider re-profiling the margins to shallow slopes (maximum 1 in 3). All debris should be removed well off site, although ideally any aquatic vegetation should be left close to the water's edge for at least a few hours to allow larvae and other animals to return to water.

Rivers, streams and ditches

Agricultural, sewage and industrial pollution prevent all but a few tolerant dragonfly species, if any, from living in many watercourses. Water quality is the joint responsibility of the EA/SEPA/

DoE(NI), water companies, industry, farmers and other landowners, all of whom can also help to restore degraded waters. The effects of pollution are greatest in small watercourses. Farmers are encouraged to follow the Defra Codes of Good Agricultural Practice (Defra, 1998) and, in so doing, should prevent pollution by farm wastes, fertilisers and pesticides.

Overgrown watercourses may be used by a few specialist dragonflies, while newly-cleared ones attract others. Therefore, clearance operations should aim to provide a range of conditions by dredging or clearing weeds, on a rotation, from no more than a quarter of the banks in any one year. The provision of a ledge, or berm, at the base of one bank allows marginal plants to flourish without greatly affecting water flow. After clearance, recolonisation by plants and animals occurs from nearby undisturbed stretches. Therefore, treated lengths should be as short as possible and never more than 400 m. In the case of ditch management, the ideal would be to manage alternate 30 m stretches on one side of the bank in any one year.

The length of the ditch management rotation depends on factors such as aquatic vegetation growth rates, whether the ditches have an important water transport or livestock control function, or the type of grazing animal present. Possible options for drainage channel cleaning cycles are:

- light maintenance every year
- a two-year cycle, cutting half the channel width each year
- less frequent routine maintenance with targeted control of emergents more often as necessary
- radical cleaning of 10–20% of the ditches every year.

The greatest diversity of aquatic plants is most often associated with freshwater ditches managed every three to five years. Drainage channels on peat may have to be cleaned frequently if they are subject to subsidence and are essential as wet fences. Brackish ditches require less maintenance and can be managed on a ten-year rotation. There may be some ditches that serve no drainage function that can be allowed to mature for even longer periods.

David Smallshire

Plate 10.2
Banded demoiselle

When clearing out watercourses:

- Leave spoil on the bankside for several hours before spreading to allow invertebrates and amphibians to return to the water.
- Deposit spoil away from the bank in areas of low wildlife interest and where sediment and nutrients from rotting plants do not feed directly into a watercourse. Avoid smothering important bank side and field habitats. A muck-spreader can be used to scatter the spoil widely.
- Ensure that livestock do not have access to spoil that may contain poisonous plant matter (eg hemlock, iris and water-dropworts).

Excessive plant growth indicates nutrient enrichment. If the source of this cannot be traced and controlled, and mechanical clearance is impractical, herbicides may be used as a last resort. However, only cleared products may be applied and only by qualified personnel, and approval must be sought from the EA, SEPA or DoE(NI). Only short lengths should be treated at any one time; where possible treat the two sides of a watercourse in different years, leaving at least two years between treatments.

Many watercourses have little marginal vegetation in which adult dragonflies may feed and roost. Where this is due to cropping or grazing close to the watercourse, there are additional threats from fertiliser and pesticide drift and erosion by livestock. In such cases, these threats can be reduced by providing unfarmed buffer strips, ideally at least 10 m wide and densely vegetated. Unmown vegetation on river and ditch banks provides important shelter for many insects. This should be retained until late autumn, if possible. It is beneficial to have some dappled shade over watercourses, if necessary by planting some broadleaved shrubs and trees such as alder and willow. However, conifers should be avoided within 50 m of watercourses, as run-off may alter water chemistry and hence eliminate some aquatic life.

Small watercourses are especially prone to drying out, which may be catastrophic for aquatic life. If the cause is water abstraction, steps should be taken to control it before they dry out. In other cases, a temporary dam or sluice may help to retain water until levels rise naturally.

Wetland habitats can be created or enhanced by creating new ditches, provided that this is not detrimental to the existing habitat. The physical disturbance of creating new ditches can release soil nutrients and enrich the water. Therefore, newly created ditches should not be connected up to existing ditches or water bodies of nature conservation significance until their nutrient status has stabilised. This may take up to three years.

Ditches that maximise water flow tend to be the least beneficial for wildlife, and are characterised by steep sides. They also require more frequent management as the edges are more liable to collapse, particularly where livestock have access. Re-profiling banks to provide slopes of less than 1 in 2 allows growth of emergent plants, enables cattle to drink without falling in and provides habitat for invertebrates and feeding areas for waders and their chicks. Flow rates should not be heavily compromised, provided that ditches are kept to a depth of more than 1 m.

Agri-environment schemes

You may be eligible to receive payments for the following options that will benefit invertebrates in ponds and ditches:

- rotational ditch management
- buffering waterbodies, watercourses and ditches from pesticide and fertiliser inputs and soil erosion, and establishing buffer strip vegetation
- maintenance of ponds of high wildlife value
- management of wet grassland
- raising water levels.

In England, the Single Payment Scheme requires farmers not to cultivate within 2 m of the centre of a watercourse and within 1 m of the top of a watercourse bank.

Further reading

Brooks S (ed.) (2002) *Field guide to the dragonflies and damselflies of Great Britain and Ireland*. British Wildlife Publishing, Hook.

Kirby P (2001) *Habitat management for invertebrates: a practical handbook*. The RSPB, Sandy.

MAFF (1995) *Guidelines for the use of herbicides in or near water*. Defra publications.

Smallshire D and Swash A (2004) *Britain's dragonflies*. WILDGuides, Old Basing, UK.

Useful websites

British Dragonfly Society: www.dragonflysoc.org.uk

Buglife – the Invertebrate Conservation Trust: www.buglife.org.uk

Centre for Aquatic Plant Management – www.nerc-wallingford.ac.uk/research/capm/index.htm

Environment Agency: www.environment-agency.gov.uk

Ponds Conservation Trust: http://www.brookes.ac.uk/other/oldpondaction_250102/index.htm

11 Bumblebees and other pollinating insects

11.1 Introduction

Bumblebees are social bees of the genus *Bombus*, of which there are 27 species known from the UK. They are major pollinators of a large number of wild flowers, and of a number of crops including oilseed rape, field beans, sunflowers, peas, runner beans, raspberries, strawberries, apples and currants. The degree of dependency on bumblebees varies greatly; some crops such as field and runner beans are exclusively dependent on bumblebees, while other such as oilseed rape are also pollinated by other insects and/or the wind. There is evidence that yield of field beans drops due to inadequate pollination when field size exceeds 12 ha.

There are many other pollinating insects in the UK, best known of which is the honeybee, kept in domestic hives and also found as feral nests. In addition there are well over 200 other species of solitary bee found in the UK, most of which are small and rarely noticed but many of which are valuable pollinators. All bees feed exclusively on nectar and pollen that they collect from flowers. More broadly, many other insects visits flowers and provide something in the way of pollination services, including hoverflies (Syrphidae), various other flies (Diptera) and butterflies and moths (Lepidoptera). In total, the value of pollinating insects to European agriculture has been estimated at around 5 billion Euros.

Bumblebees have an annual life cycle, with mated queens emerging from hibernation in late winter or spring. They search for nest sites, and found a nest in which they initially rear workers (daughters). When they are adult the workers take over foraging duties and the queens never again leave their nest. The nest grows through the spring and early summer, and in some species may contain up to 400 workers by July. In mid- to late summer the nest produces new queens and males, which leave the nest to mate. The new queens rapidly enter hibernation after mating. They hibernate a few centimetres below the soil surface. The workers, males and the old queen die off in late summer.

11.2 Populations and distribution

Bumblebees are broadly distributed across the temperate and montane regions of the northern hemisphere. Within the UK, some bumblebee species can be found in all regions. Some species are at the northern edge of their range in the UK, and so are more abundant in the south (such as the ruderal bumblebee). Unusually for an insect group, several species are towards the southern edge of their range in the UK and thus have northerly distributions; Scotland holds the bulk of the remaining populations of five UK bumblebee species.

A majority of bumblebee species have undergone dramatic declines across the UK, and also in Western Europe and North America. Of the 27 UK species, three have gone extinct in the UK. A further eight species have undergone major range contractions, and two of these, the shrill carder bee and the great yellow bumblebee, are severely threatened in the UK. Declines have occurred most in the

Plate 11.1 The shrill carder bee, the rarest surviving bumblebee species in lowland England.

lowlands, particularly south, east and central England, areas where farming is particularly intensive. Thus species with southerly distributions have been most hard hit (this group includes the three species to have gone extinct in the UK). Although historical data on abundance and distributions are sparse, declines in bumblebee range and abundance have probably been going on for c60 years, and recent evidence suggests that they are continuing.

The social nature of bumblebees renders them particularly susceptible to habitat loss. The vast majority of bees seen on the wing are workers, which are sterile. The breeding unit for bumblebees is the nest, which contains just one breeding female, the queen. Workers can travel for more than 1 km from the nest in search of food. Each nest probably requires several hectares of good foraging habitat within flight range. Since a viable population must contain a minimum of around 50 nests, in total this requires a substantial area of flower-rich habitat. Nature reserves in the UK are too small to support viable populations of rare bumblebees. If we are to ensure that these species survive, it is vital that we provide more flowers in the farmed countryside.

Honeybees are domesticated rather than primarily wild organisms, and so are not of conservation concern. There is currently some debate as to whether other groups of pollinators such as hoverflies have declined significantly. Data are too few to be sure, but it seems highly likely that numbers of at least some species have declined in intensively farmed areas.

Factors affecting populations on lowland farmland

Bumblebees have been particularly hit by loss of unimproved grasslands (chalk downland, hay meadows etc), of which the UK has lost about 98%. Conversion of grazed downland to cereal production, and the switch from hay production from flower-rich meadows to silage production from grass monocultures have both greatly reduced flower availability in the agricultural landscape. Also abandonment

Plate 11.2
The buff-tailed bumblebee, one of few species which remain relatively common across the UK.

of clover leys, once an important part of crop rotations in some regions, has undoubtedly had a major impact (in parts of Eastern Europe where they are still used they are a major food source for bumblebees). Removal of hedgerows and increases in field sizes are likely to be contributing factors, for hedges and adjacent margins provide both flowers and nesting sites. Drift of herbicides and fertiliser runoff into field margins are also likely to have negatively impacted on wildflower populations.

Overall, these changes have resulted in significant declines in many wildflower species on which bumblebees depend. Red clover in particular is much less abundant than formerly, and is a major source of both nectar and pollen for the endangered long-tongued bumblebee species. Most authorities agree that it is probably declines in wildflower abundance that is the primary factor driving declines in bee numbers.

Nests of carder bumblebee that are above ground are susceptible to damage from farming operations, particularly cutting and mowing. The switch from hay to silage production has probably been damaging to these species since silage is cut much more frequently than hay. It is likely that many nests are destroyed each year in this way.

It is unclear how damaging direct effects of insecticides have been for bumblebees, although there are some isolated records of significant mortality. Unlike honeybees, bumblebees often forage until late in the evening, so it is difficult to time applications to avoid their foraging period. The only option is thus to avoid spraying areas where there are flowers.

11.3 Habitat requirements

To flourish, bumblebees require an adequate supply of suitable flowers, and undisturbed places to nest and to hibernate. Different species tend to feed on different flowers, in part reflecting differences in tongue length. Species with short tongues tend to feed on shallow flowers (eg bramble), those with long-tongues on deep flowers such as foxglove, honeysuckle or red clover. Overall, bumblebees tend to prefer biennial and perennial herbaceous plants, and with some exceptions they tend to avoid annual flowers, most of which provide little nectar. Fabaceae (the pea family which includes clovers, trefoils, vetches etc) are particularly important as a source of protein-rich pollen needed to feed the larvae. The bumblebee species that have declined most in recent decades tend to be long-tongued, and these species are especially dependent on Fabaceae.

Different bumblebee species tend to nest in different places. Some species, notably the carder bumblebees, nest just above the ground in dense tussocky grass, and thus require undisturbed grassland or field margins where grass tussocks are allowed to form. Most other species nest below

Plates 11.3 and 11.4 Two examples of flower-rich unimproved grassland, idea habitat for bumblebees: chalk downland in Hampshire (top); coastal machair on South Uist, Hebrides (bottom).

ground, often using abandoned burrows of rodents. Tillage removes such holes so once again undisturbed ground is needed for nesting. In agricultural landscapes the majority of nests of both groups tend to be along linear features such as hedges or fence lines.

Little is known about bumblebee hibernation sites, but they certainly need undisturbed soil, and are said to prefer north-facing banks. It is likely that areas suitable for nesting (hedgerows, uncultivated field margins etc) are also suitable for hibernation.

Table 11.1 Suitable wildflowers for bumblebees.

Anthyllis vulneraria	Kidney vetch
Ballota nigra	Black horehound
Centaurea spp.	Knapweeds
Dipsacus fullonum	Teasel
Digitalis purpureum	Foxglove
Echium vulgare	Viper's bugloss
Lamium album	White deadnettle
Lotus corniculatus	Bird's-foot-trefoil
Odonites vernus	Red bartsia
Onobrychis viciifolia	Sainfoin
Papaver rhoeas	Poppy
Rhinanthus minor	Yellow rattle
Rubus fruticosus	Bramble
Stachys spp.	Woundworts
Symphytum officinalis	Comfrey
Trifolium repens	White clover
Trifolium pratense	Red clover
Vicia cracca	Tufted vetch

11.4 Management advice

A number of options are available to encourage bumblebees in farmland. Simple measures include avoiding ploughing close to field margins to leave a strip of undisturbed ground which will provide both nest sites and some wildflowers. Similarly leaving field corners undisturbed will serve the same function. Where grass mixes are sown in field margins, there is added benefit from including wild flowers that can survive within a grass sward, such as knapweed, scabious, clovers and bird's-foot-trefoil. Cutting hedges every second year allows bramble and hedgerow shrubs to flower. Thick hedges are better because they support more small mammals and thus are more likely to provide more bumblebee nest sites. Conservation headlands (with reduced or no spraying) will reduce herbicide and insecticide penetration into hedge bases. Areas of deciduous woodland (even very small ones) are of value in providing spring forage (eg bluebells, sallow) and undisturbed nesting areas. Traditional orchards in which a diverse ground flora has been allowed to developed can provide excellent bumblebee habitat. In Germany established low-density orchards which are also periodically cut for hay support a diverse bumblebee assemblage including very rare species such as the short-haired bumblebee (now extinct in the UK).

Peter Creed

Plate 11.5 Common knapweed (rayed form)

Uncropped field margins are of limited value for bumblebees if they are tilled annually since they encourage only annual flowers which are generally avoided by bumblebees. If left untilled for longer periods, communities of perennial flowers will eventually establish and provide good bumblebee habitat, but the time this takes will depend on the local seed bank. A swifter option is to sow a pollen and nectar wildflower seed mix now available under agri-environment schemes such as the Environmental Stewardship scheme in England. This mix includes clovers, bird's-foot-trefoil and knapweed, all excellent flowers for bumblebees. Whatever the method of establishment, these areas will need occasional mowing to prevent scrub establishment. Cutting in September/ October minimises impact on pollinator populations. Research has shown that cutting around late May/early June will promote late flowering of some species in the mix and in particular red clover, which is a major source of nectar for bumblebees. To extend the foraging period, it is important that no more than half of the area is cut at this time, with the cutter no lower than 20 cm.

Similar comments apply to set-aside; long-term set-aside could provide suitable habitat for bumblebees, but is of greatly reduced value if it is topped each year in midsummer (this removes all the flowers). If topping is required, cutting as close to the 15 August deadline as possible is beneficial since by this time many bumblebee nests will have already finished. Also make use of the option to leave 25% of the area uncut for up to three years.

In some areas agri-environment schemes may be available for the restoration of flower-rich lowland hay meadows or chalk downland. In the long term, these will provide perfect habitat for bumblebees. However, it is important that they be grazed little or not at all in summer, since most grazing animals (especially sheep) preferentially eat the flowers first. Sheep can strip all of the flowers from a field in a few hours. Light grazing in winter, especially by cattle, is beneficial.

Any opportunity to incorporate leguminous ley crops into the farming system would provide great benefits for bumblebees. Clovers (especially red and zig-zag), trefoils and sainfoin all provide excellent bumblebee forage.

Use of commercially reared bumblebee nests

It should be noted that in recent years many nests of the buff-tailed bumblebee have been imported to the UK, primarily for pollination of glasshouse tomatoes but increasingly to boost pollination of outdoor fruit crops such as strawberries. The strain being imported is not native to the UK, originating from southern Europe. There is a danger that these bees might interbreed with our native bees, or contaminate our native bee populations with diseases from abroad. The importation is in contravention of the Wildlife and Countryside Act.

Further reading

Goulson D (2003) *Bumblebees; their behaviour and ecology*. Oxford University Press.

Prys-Jones E and Corbet S A (1991) *Bumblebees*. Richmond Publishing Co. Ltd.

Further information

More information and advice on how best to manage farmland for bumblebees can be obtained from the Bumblebee Conservation Trust, (www.bumblebeeconservationtrust.co.uk), School of Biological and Environmental Sciences, University of Stirling, Stirling, FK9 4LA.

12 Beneficial insects and spiders of arable farmland

12.1 Introduction

Arable fields are home to between 1,500–3,000 different species of insects and spiders, many of which are beneficial, helping to control pests, pollinate flowers or assist with the breakdown of organic matter. These insects are also an essential food source for other farmland wildlife including birds, bats, small mammals, amphibians and reptiles. This chapter covers the predatory and parasitic insects and spiders (beneficial arthropods) that aid pest control in arable crops. Of those insects that feed on crops, relatively few ever cause economically important damage because their numbers are controlled by an army of beneficial arthropods and it is only when conditions occur that heavily favour the pest or their predators are reduced by agricultural operations, that pest outbreaks develop.

12.2 Populations

The only long-term evaluation of arthropod numbers within arable crops is that conducted by The Game Conservancy Trust on the Sussex Downs. This revealed a 57% decline in the overall abundance of arthropods from 1970 to 1985, followed by some recovery so that the current abundance is 43% of that in 1970. A wide spectrum of arthropod families were monitored and a range of population changes were found, from consistent declines to steady increases. Polyphagous predators have decline steadily since 1970 (Figure 12.1), with Staphylinidae (rove beetles) showing the sharpest decline (Figure 12.2). The Braconidae which are

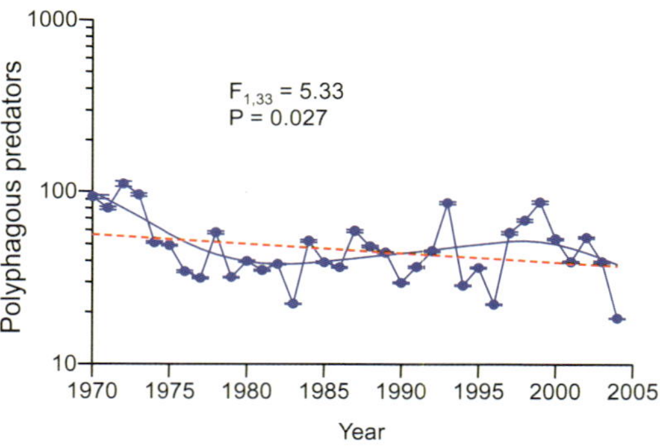

Figure 12.1
Population changes of polyphagous predators, 1970–2005.

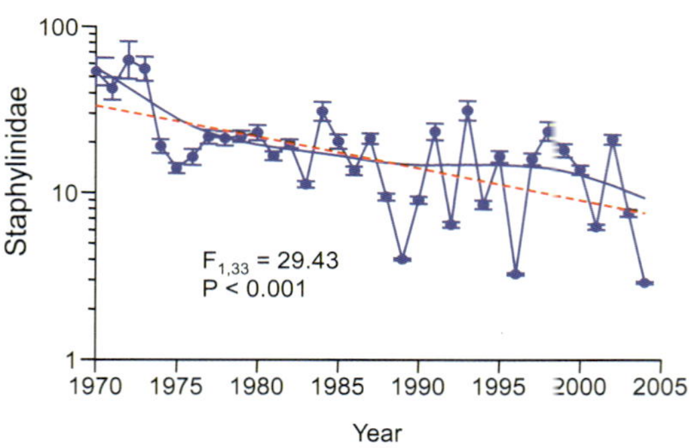

Figure 12.2
Population changes of rove beetles Staphylinidae, 1970–2005.

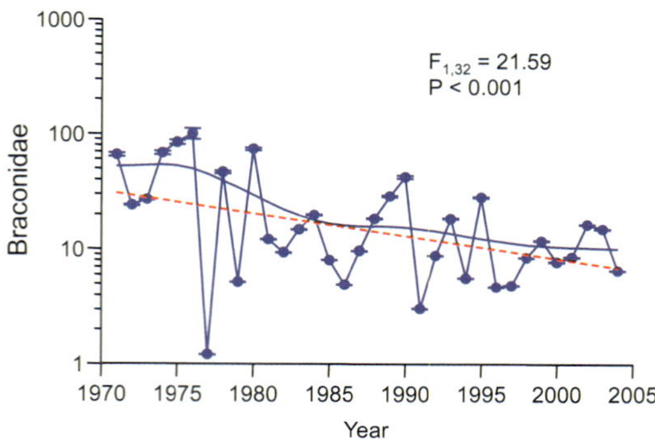

Figure 12.3
Population changes of Braconidae, 1970–2005.

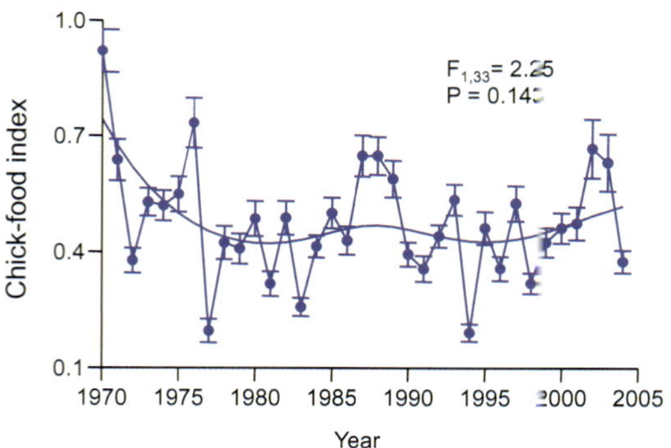

Figure 12.4
Chick-food index, 1970–2005.

largely parasitic on cereal aphids have also declined markedly (Figure 12.3). The chick-food index provides a measure of arthropods important in the diet of the grey partridge chicks and although this declined until 1990 there is some evidence of a recovery (Figure 12.4). The distribution of species across the 64 km^2 study area has also changed with many taxa becoming less widespread, except in the areas where mixed farming has remained.

12.3 Types of beneficial arthropods

Predatory insects and spiders

Within an arable crop there can be at least 400 predatory species comprised largely of beetles (Coleoptera), spiders (Araneae), mites (Acari), true bugs (Hemiptera), flies (Diptera) and harvestmen (Opoliones). These are often referred to as generalist predators and they have diverse diets and feeding habits. Some of the beetles are capable of climbing plants in search of their prey, but the majority have been shown to be opportunistic scavengers consuming a wide variety of prey found at ground level. As most pests spend a proportion of their lifetime on or in the ground they are highly vulnerable to this type of foraging. Predators may make use of pollen and nectar if insect prey are scarce. Some of the predatory insects specialise in feeding on one type of prey, the most well known are those that feed on aphids such as the ladybirds (Coccinellidae), hoverflies (Syrphidae) and lacewings (Chrysopidae). However, the diet of the different life-stages may vary, especially with the flying predators. The larvae of hoverflies and lacewings are predatory but the adults feed upon pollen and nectar.

The wide diversity of predators found in arable crops ensures that most microhabitats within the crop and its surrounding environment are home to some predatory species. The most intensively studied groups of predatory arthropods are the beetles and spiders and much is now known about their life-cycles, habitat requirements and diet. These are also the most numerically important and most diverse group of predators. They vary considerable in their ecology; some reside all year within the field, such as the frequently found ground beetle *Pterostichus melanarius*, whereas other species only occupy the field for part of their lifecycle, inhabiting field margins or other non-crop areas for the remainder of the time. The diversity of predators is always highest around the edges of fields, especially within 60 m, declining sharply further into the field. This is because some species utilise the resources provided by margins throughout the year, others are more closely associated with weeds that are also more abundant near field edges or they are incapable of dispersing far from the boundaries. Although most predators are capable of flight, the extent to which they disperse varies considerably with some of the less mobile ground beetles moving less than a couple of hundred metres in their lifetime. In contrast, the money spiders and hoverflies can travel hundreds of kilometres before selecting an appropriate crop. Their relative mobility is important because it influences their rate of recovery following disruption by agricultural practices such as soil tillage and insecticide applications. Thus it is not only how the crop environment is managed but also the immediate surrounding habitats that will influence the abundance and diversity of beneficial arthropods and thereby the level of pest control. Indeed, the whole farm landscape and proportion of non-crop areas within that has been shown to influence natural pest control. Consequently the ideal

Roy Anderson

Plate 12.1 The ground beetle *Pterostichus melanarius.*

landscape is one comprised of a mosaic of different crops and non-crop areas which will ensure habitat diversity is sufficient to support high and diverse populations of beneficial arthropods.

Parasitic insects

One quarter of all insects are parasitic and these are prevalent in agroecosystems, with annual crop pests having at least two parasitoid species attacking them and often more. As the parasitoids feeding upon their host cause its death, they can aid pest control. Parasitoids vary in the number of pest species that they can parasitise, the most adaptable being able to attack a wide range of pests found on a large variety of food plants. Because of the ephemeral nature of arable crops and their pests, the more specialist parasitoids have to follow their hosts dispersal pattern and may need to move between the crop and non-crop areas. Thus, as for many predatory species, parasitoids can also be found overwintering in non-crop areas along with their hosts, moving into the crop in the spring. It is not known how far they are capable of dispersing, although they can be carried long distances by the wind. Parasitoids also respond to chemical cues when locating their host, the host's food plant and each other, therefore, they have some control over their more localised movements.

A source of nectar is important to most parasitoids, as the nutrients this provides controls many aspects of their biology including their life expectancy and reproductive capability. Provision of extra floral resources in habitats where they are scarce is considered to increase the levels of pest parasitism.

Plate 12.2 *Aphelinus* ovipositing in an aphid.

Syngenta Bioline

Other farmland insects

Many other insect species occur in crops and their field boundaries that are also important to the farmland ecosystem. Some of these species may feed on weeds and their seeds thereby reducing the need for weed control. Insects along with rodents and birds are the main consumers of weed seeds, the insects feeding on the smaller species (eg chickweed, shepherd's-purse and field poppy) and rodents the larger ones (eg wild oats, knotgrass, orache and fat-hen). Ground beetles and ants are the arthropods that feed most on weed seeds. Levels of seed consumption by invertebrates are highest during the spring and summer when they are most active, while rodents and birds consume more seeds in the autumn and winter. Field studies have shown that 100% of the available seeds can be consumed or damaged by these predators within a few days. The impact of species feeding on weed leaves and roots has not been studied to any great extent. Others insects consume fungi on plants or in the soil and may help with crop disease control.

The soil is host to a whole myriad of insects that feed upon detritus, fungi, nematodes and other soil organisms, with many contributing substantially to nutrient recycling whilst also acting as a source of food for organisms higher in the food chain. A fully functioning soil can help maintain soil structure, ensure nutrient recycling and the breakdown of pesticides, leading to less off-farm pollution whilst also helping to contain damaging pests and diseases. This is best achieved by increasing soil organic matter and reducing the intensity and frequency of soil cultivations

Insects as food

Insects are a rich source of protein and consequently they are consumed by birds, bats, small mammals, amphibians and

Steve Moreby

Plate 12.3
A range of insects found in the diet of chicks.

reptiles. The importance of insects in the diet of farmland birds was first highlighted by The Game Conservancy Trust in their studies of the grey partridge in the 1970s. Since then the supply of insects has been linked to the survival of other farmland birds including corn bunting, yellowhammer and skylark. As the diet of most farmland songbirds is similar, having an adequate supply of insects for chicks is likely to be crucial for a wider range of species. The groups of insects that were most frequently found in the diet of chicks were the adults of beetles, bugs, flies, butterflies, moths, ants and spiders, along with the larvae of butterflies, moths and flies. These arthropods are also consumed outside of the breeding season but most birds also consume other types of food and so are less dependent on insects. The survival of bats, amphibians and reptiles is highly dependent on their being a sufficient supply of arthropods, and are also an important dietary component for hedgehogs, foxes, badgers and many rodent species.

12.4 Management advice

Crop management

To ensure that consistent and acceptable levels of pest control are achieved it is necessary to maximise the proportion of the pests life that is attacked by natural enemies. The greater the diversity of habitats that abound in an agro-ecosystem the greater the number and diversity of beneficial insects and this leads to better and more reliable pest control. More diverse habitats also provide a wider range of environmental conditions and ensure that a diverse supply of alternative prey are available for periods when pests are low.

The abundance, diversity and distribution of beneficial arthropods within arable farmland are determined by a range of farming practices while climatic factors and the surrounding landscape will buffer these impacts. Within the field, the type of crop and the husbandry practices associated with it will determine its suitability in terms of habitat and prey availability, but also how it impacts on the beneficial arthropod's lifecycle. The practices known to have the largest impact are soil cultivations, insecticide and herbicide inputs and, associated with these, the crop type. The largest differences occur between winter-sown cereal crops and spring-sown root crops, the latter usually being associated with more intensive soil cultivations in the spring, later development of ground cover and often greater pesticide applications. Consequently, root crops have generally been found to harbour fewest beneficial arthropods. Following agricultural operations that reduce beneficial arthropods, there will be recolonisation from surrounding untreated fields and non-crop habitats but the speed of recovery depends on the size of the affected area. Thus if many adjacent fields contain the same crop (block cropping), recovery will be slower, increasing the chance that pest populations will increase in the absence of their predators and parasites. Having a diverse mixture of crops in a locality will also encourage a greater diversity of beneficial arthropods, lowering the risk of an initial pest outbreak.

Soil management
Extremely high numbers of beneficial arthropods overwinter within fields, including beetles, flies and spiders, along

with parasitoids overwintering within their pest host. The density of beetles alone was found to be 1.5 million per hectare. These arthropods are vulnerable to the type and timing of soil cultivations; ploughing and power harrows can cause physical damage while also exposing them to predators, with less pronounced effects in lighter compared to heavy soils. Adopting non-inversion tillage practices allows more beneficial arthropods to survive and in the longer-term, because the soil organic matter builds-up near the surface encouraging fungal and detritus feeding arthropods, such as springtails (Collembola) along with earthworms, there is more alternative prey for beneficial arthropods allowing their populations to build. The timing of cultivations and subsequent seedbed preparations may also influence arthropod survival and it is likely that a combination of these factors, in addition to crop type and its associated pesticide use, will determine the ultimate arthropod population. Likewise, the undersowing of cereal crops prior to the establishment of a grass ley also benefits arthropods, because the soil remains undisturbed through the winter. In addition, the young grass supports chick food insects, especially sawflies.

The application of organic manures have also been shown to be of benefit because they encourage fungi and detritus feeding species which then act as additional food for beneficial arthropods.

Insecticides

Insecticides and some molluscicides have been shown to reduce beneficial arthropods, directly by causing mortality and indirectly by for example reducing reproductive rates or by reducing their activity and increasing the chance of predation. Some species can reinvade the treated field after an insecticide application if surrounding crops and non-crop remain untreated. However, for those species residing permanently within fields or with low dispersal ability then recovery may not occur during the current season and reductions can persist into the following year. If the insecticide fails to control the pest but removes the predators then a more severe pest outbreak can occur either in that season or the following one. This is more likely to occur with pests that are difficult to control, these being the ones that are only vulnerable to insecticides for a short period of their lifecycle (eg orange wheat blossom midge) or are becoming resistant to insecticides (eg peach potato aphid).

The first step to reduce the impact of insecticides is to ensure they are only applied when absolutely necessary and this relies on there being a good understanding of the relationship between pest abundance and economic damage, from which a spray threshold can be determined. Monitoring pest levels and only applying insecticides when this threshold is reached will reduce unnecessary applications. Pests may also occur in patches within fields and not all fields may be infested, therefore targeting applications only to areas where damage thresholds have been exceeded will also help to preserve beneficial insects and save on insecticide costs.

The choice of insecticide is also important, using selective insecticides and reducing the number and dosage of broad-spectrum insecticides will reduce their impact, and this is especially important during the spring and early summer when arthropod activity is at its peak. Of the insecticides available, the organophosphates and pyrethroids have a broad-spectrum of action and will cause high mortalities of most beneficial insects. The carbamate insecticide pirimicarb is the most selective, sparing many beneficial species. New application technology can also ensure insecticides are applied accurately, thereby reducing drift to non-crop areas and avoiding over-dosing within the crop.

Herbicides

Herbicides can also affect the numbers of beneficial insects indirectly through removal of host plants and by the creation of monocultures. Weeds provide a wide range of alternative food resources, attracting phytophagous insects and producing nectar, pollen and seed that is food for beneficial arthropods. They also create more diverse habitats and microclimates that support a wider range of beneficial arthropods. The creation of a weedier environment within the crop can be achieved by adopting a herbicide regime that allows some of the less competitive weeds to survive. This may include the use of selective herbicides, lower dosages and patch spraying of the more noxious weeds. Around field edges such an approach can be funded by implementing conservation headlands. These have been shown to increase beneficial arthropod abundance and diversity sufficiently to increase the survival of farmland birds such as the grey partridge. Moreover, levels of pest control were also improved in the adjacent crop because the weeds were providing nectar that was used by hoverflies and ground beetles were better fed increasing their reproductive rate. The agri-environment schemes also have low-input crop options where whole crops can be managed under this regime. Including this option within a rotation can help to build beneficial arthropod populations.

Overwintered stubbles
Following harvest, insects that overwinter in the surrounding margins will start to leave the field and consequently their survival will be much higher if the field remains uncultivated through the autumn. Seeds will also remain available on the surface for insects, birds and small mammals. If weedy stubbles are created by not pre- or post-harvest herbicides, these will support plant-feeding insects so providing more food resources for predators. Spiders in particular will be encouraged by the more diverse structure created by weeds and crop debris. Adoption of non-inversion tillage can have similar benefits and in cereal crops can reduce aphids infestations in the autumn.

Habitat management

Some beneficial arthropods frequent habitats outside of the crop for foraging, breeding and surviving dormant periods (eg overwintering). Flower strips and grass strips are two approaches that supplement these requirements and have been widely investigated with respect to their impact on beneficial arthropods within adjacent crops.

Flower strips
A range of beneficial arthropods, especially hoverflies and parasitoids make use of pollen and nectar. In addition, the plants also support a diverse community of other insects including pollinators that can increase crop yields (bees, butterflies, flies) or herbivorous insects that act as an alternative food supply for the predatory arthropods.

Flowering plants should be selected so that they provide a sequential supply of pollen and nectar from spring to early autumn. Flowers with a simple, open structure that allow access to the nectar should be used to encourage predatory and parasitic insects because they do not posses specialised nectar feeding mouthparts. On farmland, parasitoids were found to prefer simple open flowers such as those of wild carrot, hogweed, cow parsley and angelica. Likewise, hoverflies also congregated on such flowers along with those of yarrow. Flowers with more complex structures can be added to attract a more diverse range of bee species.

Flower-rich margins are often created by establishing a mix of fine grasses and flowering plants able to survive in a grass

Tom Birkett

Plate 12.4 Hoverflies on thistle

Plate 12.5 Flower-rich field margin

sward (eg knapweed, scabious, yarrow and bird's-foot-trefoil) or by creating a specific pollen and nectar mix of clovers and vetches. Fine grasses are included as these can aid establishment and weed control, but these grasses can also outcompete the pollen and nectar sources and reduce the lifespan of the mix. Grasses are, however, an important food source for many of the insects that use the pollen and nectar source, but this can also be provided in adjacent buffer strips rather than the mix itself. The choice of flowering plant species included in such mixes is usually based upon their attractiveness to pollinators, but flowers with more open structures (as listed above) should also be included if beneficial insects for pest control are to be attracted. Annuals can also be used to create flower-rich areas and have the advantage that such areas can be rotated with the crops. Plants that are suitable for such purpose include phacelia, buckwheat, dill and coriander.

Plate 12.6 Phacelia, rich in pollen and nectar

Grass buffer strips and beetle banks

Beetles and spiders overwinter within tussocky grasses because these provide stable environmental conditions through cold periods. However, fields cannot be too large because most of the species overwintering within them disperse by walking and adequate pest control will only be achieved if they are spread across the field when the pests start to build up in the spring. In fields greater than 16 ha, unless they are particularly narrow, it is beneficial to divide them using beetle banks – raised strips created by ploughing inwards from each side and sown with a tussocky grass mix. The bank is generally 2 m wide, but wider features can accommodate more overwintering predators and are better buffered from sprays, so beetle banks with wildbird cover strips either side are even better. Having no more than 120 m between beetle banks is considered ideal. Whilst the tussocks are the essential feature of these strips for overwintering predators, a dense tussocky margin is impenetrable to most foraging birds, but creating a diverse sward of fine and tussocky grasses will provide opportunities for a wider range of wildlife. However, the tussock-forming species should be allowed to form mature tussocks over several years, so these margins should not be cut more than once every 3–5 years, and on a rotation so that not all of the overwintering insect habitat is removed in the same year.

Suitable grassy areas may be found alongside hedgerows and ditches, where they should be protected as part of cross compliance obligations. Grass strips associated with post and wire fences are also valuable as they were found to support a higher density of overwintering beetles than hedgerow bases, although the diversity of species was lower. Additionally, rough grassland that remains ungrazed through the winter may provide a source of beneficial insects.

The value of grassy areas for beneficial insects is improved if herbaceous flowering plants are established within them, because a greater plant diversity will support a higher diversity of predatory and parasitic species, while also providing extra floral resources.

Hedgerows

Hedgerows themselves support the greatest diversity of beneficial arthropods throughout the year, the level of diversity depending on the plant composition. The number of insect species associated with different trees and shrub species can vary enormously; hawthorn supported 209 invertebrate species but holly only supported 10. A large proportion of these were found to be predatory (30%) although only 6% were parasitic. Hedgerows are also a rich source of invertebrate food for other wildlife, especially birds. Besides providing overwintering sites, structural complexity and a range of associated micro-climates, the flowering trees and shrubs in hedgerows are a source of pollen and nectar. Moreover, the hedgerow exerts an effect beyond the immediate vegetation by creating shelter, so modifying the adjacent environmental conditions and allowing a greater diversity of hedgebase plants and arthropods to exist. Hedgerows are considered to facilitate the movement of arthropods through the landscape, connecting non-crop habitats such as woodland, however only butterflies and a few beetle species have been shown to utilise them in such a manner.

Many hedgerow shrubs flower on second year wood and therefore more prolific flower production can be achieved if hedgerows are trimmed on a 2–3 year rotation (rather than annually). Their value

Plate 12.7 (left)
Beetle bank

Plate 12.8 (right)
A suitable hedgerow

John Holland

Richard Winspear/RSPB

may be further improved by having wide flower-rich margins that provide overwintering and summer foraging resources for insects. Margins by acting as a buffer zone help to protect the hedgerow from pesticide and fertiliser drift.

Bird foraging habitats

All of the above practices will support arthropods that are important in the diet of farmland birds, although not so much the plant feeding groups such as the bugs and caterpillars which feed predominantly on broadleaf weeds and grasses. Of the agri-environment options available, conservation headland and low-input cereal crops best encourage arthropods important as bird food. Gamebird and wild bird cover can also have a rich understorey of weeds. Alternatively, an insect-rich crop can also be created; plants known to support insects include a spring-sown cereal to provide vegetation for sawfly larvae and broadleaf plants such as vetches and brassicas. Covers can be funded through agri-environment schemes, sown on set-aside as a wildbird cover option or on areas eligible for the Single Farm Payment. These should be sown at a density that will allow some broadleaf weeds to emerge whilst also having an open structure to allow access for foraging birds, yet prevent predation by raptors. For both these options the area sown must be at least 6 m wide and in the case of set-aside sown next to a water-course or hedgerow. Making use of set-aside in this way can also help to alleviate the effects of block cropping, if for example a cereal based mix is sown around the edge of broadleaf crops.

Summary

How effective non-crop habitats are at improving levels of pest control also depends on the amount of non-crop habitats on the surrounding farms. Provision of additional habitats to encourage beneficial arthropods is more effective in simple landscapes, where there are large fields with few non-crop areas compared to more complex ones where there are many small fields with surrounding hedgerows, woodland and other diverse habitats. Nevertheless, to ensure that sustainable pest control is maintained it is recommended a range of practices are followed including:

- Maintaining or creating flower-rich field margins to provide nectar and pollen for a diversity of beneficial species.
- Creating raised grassy banks (beetle banks) or plant new hedgerows in fields

John Holland

Plate 12.9 Brassica is ideal for game cover.

greater than 16 ha to support large numbers of wintering beneficial arthropods which can colonise cereal crops in spring and prevent pest outbreaks.

- Avoid the use of prophylactic insecticide applications and adhere to pest spray thresholds. When insecticides are needed use selective insecticides such as pirimicarb where possible and only treat the infested area.
- Avoid complete weed control since a few weeds help provide food and habitat for wildlife including the species important in pest control. Implement conservation headlands around the edges of cereal fields.
- Adopt non-inversion soil tillage wherever possible.
- Have a diverse crop rotation and avoid block cropping.

Further reading

Gurr G M, Wratten S D, Barbosa P (2000) *Biological control: measures of success.* Kluwer Academic Publishers, Netherlands.

Holland J M (2002) *The agroecology of carabid beetles.* Intercept, Andover, UK.

Holland J M, Hutchison M A S, Smith B and Aebischer N J (2006) A review of invertebrates and seed bearing plants as food for farmland birds in Europe. *Annals of Applied Biology* 148, 49–71.

Landis D A, Wratten S D, Gurr G M (2000) Habitat management to conserve natural enemies of arthropod pests in agriculture. *Annual Review of Entomology* 45: 175–201.

Marshall E J P, Moonen A C (2002) Field margins in northern Europe: their functions and interactions with agriculture. *Agriculture, Ecosystems and Environment* 89: 5–21.

Tscharntke T, Klein A M, Kruess A, Steffan-Dewenter I, Thies C (2005) Landscape perspectives on agricultural intensification and biodiversity – ecosystem service management. *Ecology Letters* 8: 857–874.

Wackers F L, van Rijn P C and Bruin J (2005) *Plant-provided food for carnivorous insects: a protective mutualism and its applications.* Cambridge University Press, Cambridge.

Websites providing information on beneficial insects

http://www.gct.org.uk

http://www.iobc-wprs.org

http://www.soilassociation.org/web/sa/saweb.nsf/ed0930aa86103d8380256aa70054918d/67fd448ec064361080257149004cb42d!OpenDocument

http://www.biodiversitysussex.org/arable.htm

13 Soil management for the benefit of invertebrates

13.1 Introduction

The soil ecosystem has been defined as a life support system composed of air, water, minerals, flora, fauna and micro-organisms all of which interact and function together. Thus soil is a dynamic system that contains a diverse range of soil micro and macro-organisms that contribute to maintenance and improvement of soil health and structure. Soil structure, soil microbial activity and biodiversity are therefore inextricably linked and play a role in many natural processes that ultimately determine agricultural productivity. However, these processes are influenced and greatly affected by different cropping and cultivation practices.

13.2 Soil cultivation

The composition of the soil ecosystem is determined by a range of factors which include weather, climate, soil structure and texture, organic matter content, whether it is cultivated or not and even the method of cultivation employed. Consequently the farm system adopted and the crops grown will have a profound effect on the soil ecosystem. This system is likely to be most stable in permanent pasture where cultivations do not take place. In permanent grassland systems soil organic matter builds up steadily reaching a stable status where the addition of new material is matched by the decay and mineralisation of old. Additions take place from leaf and root material as well as deposition of dung from grazing livestock.

In contrast intensive arable systems involve frequent soil disturbance. The extent of this disturbance is largely dependant upon the crop being grown. For instance it is common practice when establishing oilseed rape for cultivation and crop establishment to take place simultaneously with little soil disturbance and often carried out in a single pass. Land being prepared for potatoes is initially ploughed and then subjected to a series of lighter cultivations to create a suitable tilth for bed formation. This process involves taking the soil up from the ground and separating the stones and clods of earth from the bulk of the remaining soil before returning the soil to the land. Such intensive cultivation clearly disrupts the soil ecosystem. Similarly the cultivation of soil creates an artificially porous soil structure. The increase in airspaces and the presence of oxygen amongst the soil particles causes a rapid increase in soil biological activity through the oxidation of soil organic matter. This in turn releases nutrients such as nitrates, which in turn influence soil processes. Besides altering the chemical components within the soil ecosystem, cultivation methods cause physical alterations. Where a stubble is ploughed and consolidated the fresh organic matter is moved from the biologically active soil surface to the more anaerobic section soil, often up to 20 cm deep. The actions of the machine can also affect the soil ecosystem through physically damaging the larger invertebrates, such as earthworms, and exposing them to predators. Systems which require very fine soil seedbeds, such as in the cultivation of onions and salad crops may use powered harrows or rotary cultivators which are particularly harmful to larger invertebrates.

In recent years there has been a tendency, particularly among arable farmers, to move towards less intensive cultivation systems. These are typically characterised by disc or tine based implements which, while disturb the soil, do not invert it. It is estimated that over 40% of arable soils are no longer ploughed. Retaining organic matter at the surface is beneficial to the soil ecosystem.

13.3 Soil fauna

The fauna found in soils can be divided into three basic groupings; the microfauna, the mesofauna and the macrofauna. Food and nutrient webs link all three and each contributes differently to soil biological processes.

Microfauna are generally found in the soil solution where they utilise soil organic compounds. They contribute to the formation of a stable soil structure, as filamentous fungi form a web-like net work linking soil particles. They are also responsible for much of the nutrient recycling from plant residues and soil humus and can form symbiotic liaisons with root hairs, for example mycorrhizal fungi. Other microfauna include protozoa and nematodes.

The mesofauna tend to inhabit the spaces between soil particles and aggregates. They feed upon the microfauna, mineral particles and decomposing plant material. They too assist with nutrient re-cycling and redistribution of soil organic matter. This group includes species such as mites and potworms and are an important food source for macrofaunal species.

The macrofauna live between the soil aggregates and feed on the soil substrate, soil microflora and fauna, soil organic matter and flora and fauna which inhabit above ground.

Macrofaunal species include a very wide range of invertebrate species including larval stages of moths and flies, earthworms, spiders and beetles. Some are notorious pest species of crops such as cutworms and slugs which graze the roots, stems and leaves

The SOWAP Project (SOil & WAter Protection)

A major three-year study funded by the EU LIFE programme recently reported on the interactions between soil microbial communities, erodability and tillage practices. Based on information gathered using common protocols from sites in Belgium, Hungary, UK and Czech Republic the study also included research on macrofaunal species, aquatic and terrestrial wildlife. The results from the sites showed large differences associated with season and year effects. Soil type also influenced how microbial communities reacted to tillage practice, with one of the UK sites showing an increase in soil carbon at 38% after three years of non-inversion tillage. Furthermore it was shown that a stable and larger microbial community can increase the water holding capacity of soil and a trend to a higher probability of run-off losses from soil with lower microbial biomass. Overall the project concluded that intrinsic differences exist between microbial communities that are taken from different tillage treatments. Likewise, although not always conclusively, earthworms, aquatic and terrestrial wildlife benefited from less intense tillage and the conservation of soil organic matter.

Where earthworms reach high densities with up to a kilogramme of cumulative biomass per square meter, scientists have expressed concern that this might allow compounds, such as residual herbicides, to flow more easily through the soil into the field drainage system and cause pollution. Laboratory tests using mechanically created pores indicated that this was indeed a likely occurrence. However in field trials this was not borne out as the earthworm's line the sides of their burrows with mucous and organic matter which is highly efficient in binding up pesticides.

Earthworms dislike intensive soil cultivations. This can kill, maim and expose them to predation as well as disrupting their network of burrows. Crops such as potatoes are devastating to earthworm populations but re-colonisation is surprisingly rapid, usually from the field margins, which provide a buffering and reservoir effect.

The Long Ashton LIFE Project (LA LIFE)

A 10-year study of earthworm population dynamics under two tillage regimes under the Less Intensive Farming for the Environment (UK LIFE Project) showed little differences in the first three years. After this period earthworm numbers increased overall on the less intensive plots, although there were marked differences between species, a total of 13 species being recorded.

It is clear overall that soil organic matter and tillage practices can influence soil fauna of all types and this has effects on soil erosion, soil structural stability and links up the food chain. However it is simplistic to only look at population and cultivation effects; other factors such as soil compaction, the use of manures and crop nutrients and crop protection products can all have effects.

of growing plants. Others, such as earthworms, provide an invaluable source in recycling organic matter and improving soil structure by their burrowing activities. Experimental studies have shown that up to 13 different earthworm species can be found in arable soils. Earthworms divide roughly into two groups, the deep burrowing types and the so-called net workers. The former can burrow up to 2 m deep in the soil and can form an extensive network of macro-pores. These burrows have been shown to act as an important conduit of rainfall falling on the soil surface, consequently reducing run-off and soil erosion. Soil examination pits dug in midsummer to explore crop root development show that roots are able to reach greater depths through earthworm burrows. This means that crops are able to access nutrients from depths they would not normally be able to reach but more importantly moisture, particularly in times of drought.

13.4 Soil compaction, fertilisers and pesticides

Soil over-compaction is a widespread condition caused by the application of pressure to the soil surface. This can be by driving wheels, trailed wheels, plough soles, disc edges or even by hooves of grazing livestock. The problem generally occurs when soils are soft and moist and results in the soil being reduced in volume, increased in density and less permeable to air, water and roots. Soils in this condition are likely to be more anaerobic and detrimental to soil invertebrates. Some soil types, for example heavy clays will restructure themselves naturally by cracking during the summer. However this is hindered where the crop grown in the compacted area is poor, and a lack of root development restricts water uptake and transpiration. Consequently such soils are slower to dry out. On sandy soils compaction is often associated with low organic matter levels which in turn are associated with reduced invertebrates. On such soils the compaction needs to be removed by a mechanical operation, such as ploughing.

Certain crops are also predisposed to compaction. For example the wheel rows in potato crops, or the late harvesting of crops in moist field conditions such as maize and sugar beet.

Similarly the application of organic manures can cause problems. Lack of manure and slurry storage facilities causes farmers to apply these during winter months when soils are not in a position to traffic heavy loads. Manure in itself is a highly beneficial source of organic matter which stimulates soil invertebrates, improves soil structure, porosity and condition. Other waste products such as straw, paper pulp, water pre-treatment waste, bio-solids and slurry all contribute nutrients and organic matter at varying levels. In general the higher the dry matter content the better the material is for soil conditioning, applied at the correct time of year in suitable conditions.

Inorganic fertilisers, such as Ammonium Nitrate can also be beneficial. They are usually applied from spreaders which travel down tramlines at the time of year that the soil is in better condition to cope with travelling. The dissolving and movement of nutrients into the soil may cause some short-term suppression of some soil fauna species but the nutrients themselves greatly increase crop yield and plant biomass. Where this biomass is returned to the soil it can make an important contribution to the pool of soil organic matter (SOM). Removal of crop residues, from arable farms, for use in livestock enterprises, or to be burnt in power stations, without any return depletes SOM.

Over application of such nutrients is costly both economically and environmentally. Predicting inorganic fertiliser requirements for crops is now a more scientifically accurate procedure with a number of sophisticated planning systems available.

Crop protection products applied to control pests, diseases and weeds have differing effects on soil invertebrate communities depending largely on their mode of usage. Products applied to growing crop canopies tend to affect soil invertebrates less than products incorporated into or applied onto the soil. Products with broad spectrum activity such as Methyl Bromide are likely to be extremely damaging to invertebrate communities. However these are scarcely used. The impact of broad spectrum products can be reduced by careful timing or placement. For instance, insecticidal seed treatments where a minute quantity of active ingredient is positioned precisely adjacent to the seed to protect it. Band incorporation of insecticide granules is a less precise method, but still effective. Careful choice of active ingredient can also help to reduce effects on soil invertebrates. For example slug control pellets containing Metaldehyde are specific in their role of action. They stimulate the mucous producing gland within the slug causing excessive slime production. In low moisture conditions this causes rapid dehydration and death. However, in moist conditions it is less effective and a general broader spectrum product may be required.

Summary

Soil invertebrates are at the bottom of the food web and consequently are important in agro-ecosystems. They exist as microfauna through to macrofauna and play an important role in recycling waste products, nutrients, improving soil porosity, structure and consequently productivity as well as protecting soil against erosion.

Agricultural practices can affect these communities in many ways although the precise extent depends on soil type, climate, crop type and sequence, cultivation system adopted and timing. The incorporation of crop residues, manures and other forms of organic matter as well as synthetic inputs such as crop protection products and fertilisers can also have marked beneficial and negative, but seldom irreversible effects.

14 Arable plants

14.1 Introduction

Over 150 UK plant species are characteristic of arable farmland, sharing the same ecological niche as the crop plants with which they grow. A century ago arable fields would have been one of the most vibrant displays of the British landscape, bright with yellow corn marigolds, red poppies and blue cornflowers. Farmers however, have always battled against these plants and the massive revolution in farming methods over the last 60 years has led to rapid declines, with some species 'controlled' to extinction, the elegant pink corncockle being one. A combination of the widespread use of herbicides and nitrogen fertilisers, improved seed cleaning and the development of competitive high yielding crop varieties have all contributed.

As a result of these developments, farmers today are left with a relatively small group of weeds that still can cause major crop losses, black-grass, barren brome and cleavers being three of the most persistent. These species have adapted to the changes and thrive in the nitrogen rich soil. The problems caused by pernicious species like these has made it difficult to convince farmers it is worth while conserving wild plants on arable land, but with so many species becoming very rare it is recognised that they need protection. Therefore in this chapter we are going to focus on how we put the colour back into productive arable farmland and at the same time provide food for a great many birds, insects and mammals.

Nick Jarvis

Plate 14.1 Poppies and cornflowers – the Arable Weed Project, College Lake Wildlife Centre, Buckinghamshire.

14.2 Populations and distribution

It is important to realise that, just like plant communities of grasslands and woodlands, arable plant communities have distinct relationships to soil, climate and management. Also far from being the fly-by-night colonists that some might think, arable plant communities and species show a surprisingly high fidelity to particular sites, so much so that many populations of rarer species have been recorded from specific fields for decades or even centuries. This behaviour has resulted in certain areas being particularly rich and despite all the pressures under which the arable flora has suffered; there are some areas of Britain where diverse communities of uncommon arable plants still persist. The majority have retreated from the north of the country, and with some notable exceptions, few can be found north of Yorkshire but parts of the south-east and south-west are still species-rich. Key hotspots include the chalk between Salisbury and Basingstoke, and in south Cambridgeshire. Areas around the coasts of south-west England and Wales, particularly parts of the Cornish coast are very important. The Breckland of Suffolk and Norfolk is home to an extraordinary variety of plants due to its sandy soils and warm climate, but as diverse are the heavy calcareous soils of the mid-Somerset hills.

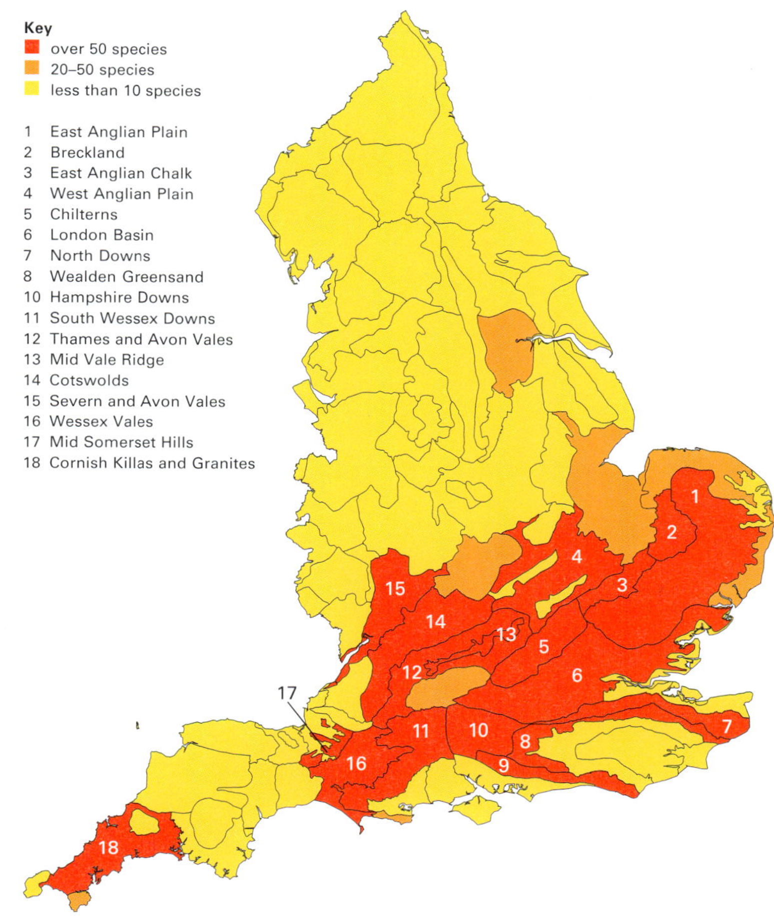

Figure 14.1
The 18 richest areas for arable plants in the UK are all in England, each with over 50 arable plant species.

Causes of decline

The decline of most arable plants, the continued persistence of others and the rise to prominence of few can be explained by their biology. The ability to form persistent seed-banks is an obvious advantage to an arable plant, and can provide a buffer against the effects of changes in arable farming practice. Many of those species that have declined so dramatically have relatively short-lived seed-banks. Corncockle, cornflower and shepherd's-needle all have short-lived seed and declined rapidly during the 1950s and 1960s, as herbicides became more effective and crops more competitive. Susceptibility to herbicides has been the main feature that has rendered species most liable to rapid decline, although their inability to compete with a highly fertilised crop has also been very important. Other factors include:

- efficient seed cleaning techniques
- the changes in crop rotation shifting from spring to autumn cultivation, leading to a loss of spring-germinating species
- the loss of certain crop types including rye and flax, which were once notorious carriers of corncockle and cornflower seed
- loss of overwintered stubbles and summer fallows
- effective field drainage minimising wet areas
- the removal of field boundaries and loss of relatively un-intensively farmed field margins
- the near complete mechanisation of farming leaving no window between harvest and ploughing for late flowering plants to grow in the stubble.

Table 14.1 Some reasons for decline of rare arable plants.

	Herbicides	Nitrogen and Competitive crops	Changes in cultivation timing	Drainage	Crop seed cleaning	Short-lived seed
Corn buttercup	**	**	*			*
Small-flowered catchfly	**	**	*			
Broad-fruited cornsalad	**	**				
Narrow-fruited cornsalad	**	**				
Cornflower	**	*			*	*
Broad-leaved cudweed	**	**				
Red-tipped cudweed	**	**				
Grass-poly	**	*		**		
Field gromwell	**		*			
Spreading hedge-parsley	**	**	**			
Red hemp-nettle	**	**	**			
Corn parsley	**	*	**			
Pheasant's-eye	**	**				
Martin's ramping-fumitory	*	*				
Shepherd's-needle	**	*				*
Fingered speedwell	*	**				
Broad-leaved spurge	**	*				
Key: ** = major factors, * = other contributing factors						

Peter Creed

Plate 14.2
Shepherd's-needle

14.3 Habitat requirements

Arable plants are well adapted to regular cultivations under traditional arable farming, but the relatively recent additions of herbicides and fertilisers, and the move to autumn-sown, dense, high-yielding crops all contribute to unsuitable growing conditions for them. Therefore, all wild plants that aspire to grow with arable crops must have a strategy not just to survive regular destruction, but also long periods when conditions are unsuitable for growth.

Like most arable crops, the majority of arable plants are annuals, which means that they complete their life-cycle within one year, and most have life-cycles that are closely synchronised with the timing of traditional arable farming. The restricted germination period of the majority of arable species, either predominantly in the late autumn and early winter or in the spring means that the plants germinating in a field in one year may be very different in another year depending on cultivation date. The long-lived seed bank of the majority of species allows this to happen as seeds can lie in waiting until the right germination conditions occur.

Land that has only been converted to arable within the last 100 years, or which is subject to repeated and heavy herbicide and fertiliser use stands little chance of supporting uncommon arable plants. Therefore particular habitat requirements that species require will include:

Peter Creed

Plate 14.3 Corn marigold

- *Farming history*: land that has a long history of continual cultivation, ideally dating back into the 19th century is likely to have more diverse plant populations.
- *Soil type*: most arable plants prefer light, well drained sandy or chalky soil that is relatively low in fertility, although some heavy soils can hold particular species of interest, eg corn buttercup.
- *Topography and aspect*: generally sites with a sunny, south-facing aspect are more species-rich, often at the top of slopes. This is due to down slope

Table 14.2 Key characteristics of rare arable plants compared with more common species.

Characteristics of rare arable plants	Characteristics of common arable plants
– Small amount of large seed produced, eg corncockle and cornflower	– Lots of small seed produced, eg shepherd's-purse and poppies
– Seed immobile	– Mobile seed
– Varied seed longevity, inversely related to seed size, eg small poppy seed is long lived but large corncockle seed only lasts for a few months	– Long-lived seed bank
– Restricted germination time	– Unrestricted germination period
– Habitat is restricted to arable land, rarely other regularly disturbed land	– Habitat will include all regularly disturbed land

erosion as a result of long periods of ploughing exposing the underlying rock and less fertile sub-soil that many species prefer.

- *Weed competition*: sites infested with cleavers, barren brome, black-grass, docks and thistles will be difficult to manage without herbicides and are unlikely to have many uncommon species as they would find it difficult to compete with the over-powering perennials and grasses.

Once a site has been identified the conditions that the arable plants will require include; annual cultivation at a time that suits the species concerned (spring or autumn), no application of herbicides (other than graminicides), fertiliser or manure and allowing plants a long enough period to flower and set seed before re-cultivating; many spring germinating species will continue flowering into late September and early October.

Table 14.3 Species characteristics

Species	Germination	Flowering	Soil Type
Broad-fruited cornsalad	Autumn	June–August	Calcareous soils and clay
Narrow-fruited cornsalad	Spring	June–August	Light calcareous loam
Corn/field gromwell	Autumn and spring	May–July	Calcareous and calcareous clay loam
Corn cleavers	Autumn	June–August	Calcareous clay loam
Mousetail	Autumn	May–July	Clay – Wet
Shepherd's-needle	Autumn and spring	May–June	Heavy calcareous clay loam
Small-flowered catchfly	Autumn and spring	June–October	Sandy loam
Spreading hedge-parsley	Autumn	July–August	Clay and calcareous clay loam
Annual knawel	Autumn	June–August	Dry, sandy, lime-free soil
Broad-leaved spurge	Autumn	June–July	Calcareous clay or silty loam
Corn parsley	Autumn (early)	July–September	Calcareous clay loam
Lesser quaking-grass	Autumn	June–August	Acidic sand and sandy loam
Corn buttercup	Autumn	May–June	Heavy clay
Corn marigold	Autumn	June–August	Sand and sandy loam
Round-leaved fluellen	Spring	July–October	Well-drained chalk
Sharp-leaved fluellen	Spring	July–October	Well-drained sand and chalk
Cornflower	Autumn	June–July	Sandy loams
Slender tare	Autumn	June–August	Calcareous clay loam
Venus's-looking-glass	Autumn and spring	May–August	Calcareous loams and calcareous clay
Night-flowering catchfly	Spring	July–September	Calcareous and calcareous sandy loams
Northern dead-nettle	Spring	May–September	Many
Red hemp-nettle	Spring	July–September	Light chalky soils
Weasel's-snout	Spring	July–September	Sandy loam and stony clay
Pheasant's-eye	Autumn and spring	June–July	Calcareous, silty and clay loam
Prickly poppy	Autumn and spring	June–July	Free-draining chalk and sandy loams
Rough poppy	Autumn and spring	June–July	Chalk loams

14.4 Management advice

It is not difficult to provide the right management conditions for arable plants. A combination of annual cultivation (either in spring or autumn depending on target species) with no fertiliser or pesticide applications will meet most plants needs. The more difficult aspects are firstly locating a rich seed bank, which will benefit from management and secondly controlling the perennial and grass weeds that will also thrive under this management.

In most fields, any remaining species-rich seed banks will be restricted to field edges, so arable plant management should normally be focused here. The rest of the crop can be managed conventionally. The first 4–6 m of the field margin is generally the lowest yielding for arable crops and so is often both the most convenient area for the farmer and the best area for arable plants. Organic farming, or other low-intensity regimes, such as summer fallows and areas managed for stone-curlews, can also enable rare arable plants to occur throughout the field.

Identify margins that meet the habitat requirements identified previously and where good variations of broadleaved 'weeds' are known to occur. Characteristic indicator species of a potentially rich arable flora include thyme-leaved sandwort, corn spurrey, common stork's-bill and loose silky-bent on sandy soils and on chalky soils venus's-looking-glass, small toadflax, fluellens and dwarf spurge.

Under agri-environment schemes, field margins can be managed in one of three ways. Firstly as conservation headlands, which are cereal field strips that are fully fertilised but only treated with highly specific herbicides, and with restrictions on fungicide and insecticide use. Conservation headlands provide excellent feeding habitat for farmland birds such as grey partridge but the application of fertiliser usually results in a competitive crop which the arable plants will find difficult to compete with so is not ideal management.

Secondly, and far more suitable are unfertilised conservation headlands which are very similar to the above but without fertiliser or manure application. These margins have been proven to be far better for arable plants as they prefer the less fertile soil and the crop and nitrogen-demanding weeds are less competitive.

Peter Creed

Peter Creed

Plate 14.4 (left) Thyme-leaved sandwort

Plate 14.5 (right) Sharp-leaved fluellen

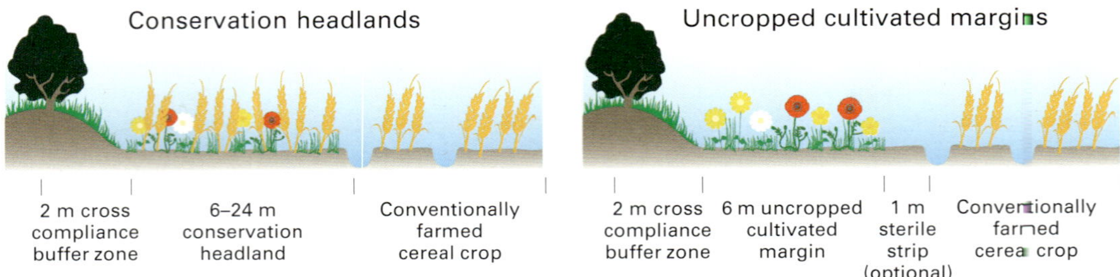

Figure 14.2
Agri-environment management options for arable plants.

Thirdly, uncropped cultivated margins provide the optimum form of management. The field margin strip is cultivated (normally at the same time as the rest of the field), but no crop is drilled and no fertilisers or pesticides are applied.

Other types of management that could benefit arable plants are:

- *Overwintered stubbles and spring cereals*: the winter stubble allows late-flowering species to set seed and autumn-germinating plants establish (particularly if a light cultivation is carried out to the stubble). The spring crop that follows will then provide an opportunity for spring germinating species and will also generally be a less intensively grown crop (eg lower fertiliser requirement and only one herbicide application).
- *Low input spring cereals* encourage more arable plant friendly conditions across the field with a spring cereal crop grown under a restricted fertiliser and herbicide programme.
- *Cultivated fallow plots for arable flora* can be placed in areas likely to benefit rare plants. Fallow plots for ground nesting birds can also provide the cultivated uncropped conditions that arable plants require.

The biggest problem with managing margins for arable plants is the risk of pernicious weeds. Controlling these weeds, notably cleavers, black-grass and barren brome, is essential if arable plants such as prickly poppy, corn marigold and weasel's-snout are to flourish.

Prevention is always the best control so cultivated margins should not be located where a known weed burden or herbicide resistance problem occurs. However, even the best sites will have some pernicious species, and if these reach a threshold which is thought damaging to either the target arable species or potentially the adjoining crop they can be controlled through cultural or chemical methods. Cultural methods are favoured; cultivation timing and depth can be altered to control particularly grass weeds. Deep ploughing (to at least 15 cm deep) will bury black-grass and barren brome seed beyond germination depth, and delaying cultivations in the autumn or waiting until spring induce seed dormancy. Introduction of occasional spring break crops into predominantly autumn-drilled crop rotations can be useful as cleavers, barren brome and black-grass are all mainly autumn germinating. It should be noted that barren brome has very little seed dormancy, helping with its cultural control.

Perennial weeds are more difficult to control by cultivation (in fact it can increase the problem by cutting and spreading roots and rhizomes) and may need selective application of herbicides. Under agri-environment scheme prescriptions herbicide use is permitted, if necessary, as either spot treatment, weed-wiping using a wick applicator, or in certain situations, boom-spraying to regain control of margins. It is far better for the conservation of arable plants if margins are treated with herbicide and re-cultivated, or moved to another site in the field, rather than to be abandoned and developed into grass buffer strips.

Weed ingress into the adjacent crop is seldom a problem as it will be receiving a complete herbicide programme but a 1 m sterile strip can be maintained between the cultivated strip and the crop to prevent the green bridge effect of weeds spreading from the hedgerow or margin.

Case Study: Ranscombe Farm, Kent

Ranscombe Farm extends to around 227 ha of the North Kent Downs, and although it is a Plantlife Nature Reserve the majority of the holding is farmed by a tenant farmer under a conventional intensive arable system. The farm has a 4-hectare Site of Special Scientific Interest (SSSI) which has been long famed amongst botanists as one of the richest sites for arable plants in the UK. The species found include hairy mallow, broad-leaved cudweed, blue pimpernel, night-flowering catchfly, narrow-fruited cornsalad and dense-flowered fumitory.

The SSSI has been subject to a management agreement for a number of years, however it has been suffering from an increase in perennial weeds including docks and couch-grass. It is thought that this problem was created during the 1990s by only carrying out shallow cultivation in the autumn. Under English Nature approval the decision was taken to spray the field with glyphosate in 2005 in an attempt to control the perennial weeds. This was carried out in September when the annuals were mainly over, but the perennials were still showing and vulnerable to herbicide. The spraying had good results, although further applications are likely to be required in future years. After spraying, the field was then cultivated in the following February. The south-facing side was ploughed but the north side still had to be disced due to practical difficulties. The combined introduction of judicious spraying and reinstatement of ploughing resulted in the reappearance of rare species such as ground pine and blue pimpernel in 2006.

In addition Ranscombe has approximately 3 km of cultivated uncropped margins, which since being established in 2004 have yielded two new populations of hairy mallow and a number of large healthy population of broad-leaved cudweed, all reappearing from seed banks. Encouraging the neighbouring farmer to carry out similar practice has resulted in a new healthy population of ground-pine.

Such instant successes as those listed above have been the result of creating straightforward uncropped, cultivated margins available under some UK agri-environment schemes at well-targeted sites, as well as reviewing management practice when it is seen to no longer be working.

Peter Creed

Peter Creed

Plate 14.6 (left)
Hairy mallow

Plate 14.7 (right)
Ground-pine

Further reading

Byfield A J, Wilson P J (2005) *Important Arable Plant Areas. Identifying priority sires for arable plants conservation in the United Kingdom*. Pp. 20. Plantlife, Salisbury.

Marshall E J P, Brown V K, Boatman N D, Lutman P J W, Squire G R, Ward L K (2003) The role of weeds in supporting biological diversity within crop fields. *Weed Research* 43: 77–89.

Walker K J, Critchley C N R, Sherwood A J, Large R, Nuttall P, Hulmes S, Rose R, Moy I, Towers J, Hadden R, Larbalestier J, Smith A, Mountford J O and Fowbert J A (2006) *Defra cereal field margin evaluation. Phase 3. Evaluation of agri-environment cultivated options in England: effectiveness of new agri-environment schemes in conserving arable plants in intensively farmed landscapes*. Pp. 73. ADAS, CEH and Defra.

Wilson P J and King M (2003) *Arable plants – a field guide*. English Nature and WildGuides, pp 312. Old Basing, Hampshire, UK. Also at www.arableplants.fieldguide.co.uk www.arableplants.org.uk

15 Plants of native or semi-natural grassland

15.1 Introduction

Semi-natural, native or unimproved grasslands, are defined as grasslands that have not been substantially modified by intensive agricultural practices and are composed of native species. These grasslands, with the exception of some acid grasslands, are rich in plant species (including grasses, herbs, sedges, rushes, mosses and liverworts) usually with at least 15 species occurring in an area of 1 m^2.

Lowland grassland is here defined as usually enclosed grasslands occurring below 300 m and excluding open grassland (rough hill grazing) above the moor wall.

Although part of the wildlife value of semi-natural grasslands is due to the association of a rich diversity of relatively widespread plants, they also support a number of threatened plant species. For example, around 54 vascular plant species typical of lowland grassland are listed as threatened and a further 27 as near threatened in the latest Red List for Great Britain.

These include some well known species or groups such as snake's-head fritillary, pasqueflower and orchids such as lesser butterfly-orchid.

A high proportion of the threatened and near threatened species (65%) are associated with calcareous grassland.

Unimproved grassland pastures can also be important for fungi, particularly species of waxcaps, earthtongues, club and coral fungi.

Peter Creed

Plate 15.1 Waxcaps in lowland pasture, Oxfordshire.

Helen Taylor

Plate 15.2 Snake's-head fritillaries, Iffley Meadows, Oxfordshire.

It should also be stressed that lowland semi-natural grasslands are also of great importance for their faunal assemblages, particularly invertebrates and birds. These topics are dealt with in previous chapters.

15.2 Grassland types and their distribution and extent

There are four broad types of semi-natural grassland that can occur in lowland farmland. These are briefly described below. Within these broad types, there are further subdivisions into specific types or communities categorised by their plant species composition as described in the National Vegetation Classification (Rodwell 1991, 1992).

Enclosed neutral hay meadows in the valleys of upland regions of the UK (upland hay meadows) are included here as a lowland grassland type.

Lowland neutral meadows and pastures

These occur on free-draining or moist neutral soils. They occur within enclosed field systems throughout the UK, normally below 300 m. They may be managed as hay meadow or as pasture. Two distinctive types are maintained by hay meadow management. One type is characteristic of lowland floodplains, largely in England. The other occurs in enclosed in-bye land in upland valleys in the northern Pennines, the Lake District and on riverbanks in Scotland.

In general, these grasslands are composed of a varied mixture of herbs, grasses and sedges with herbaceous species comprising a relatively high proportion of the sward.

Plate 15.4
Upland hay meadow, New House Meadows, North Yorkshire.

Peter Wakely, Natural England

Peter Creed

Plate 15.3
Lowland hay meadow, Wendlebury Meads, Oxfordshire.

Sarah Grinsted, Natural England

Plate 15.5 Lowland calcareous grassland, Tytherington Down, Wiltshire.

Characteristic plant species include herbs such as common knapweed, ox-eye daisy, common bird's-foot-trefoil, great burnet, lady's bedstraw, cowslip, and the grasses crested dog's-tail, quaking-grass, sweet vernal-grass, yellow oat-grass and common bent.

Lowland calcareous grassland

These occur on shallow, infertile lime-rich soils over chalk and limestone bedrock generally below 300 m throughout the UK lowlands. Many are now confined to steep valley slopes, escarpments and coastal cliffs and headlands. More rarely they may occur on level terrain such as in the East Anglian Breckland and on Salisbury Plain. A major amount of the resource is found in England (95%), particularly on the chalk.

These grasslands have a very rich flora of plants favouring lime-rich soils, including a suite of orchids. The former include common rockrose, salad burnet, small scabious, wild thyme, fairy flax and the grasses sheep's-fescue, upright brome, meadow oat-grass and crested hair-grass.

These grasslands are typically unproductive and are thus most suitable for extensive livestock grazing.

Lowland acid grassland

These occur on infertile acid soils developed over sandstones, acid igneous rocks or sands and gravels in the lowlands and upland fringes. Acid grassland is often associated with lowland dwarf shrub heath. Acid grassland can occur in a wide

Peter Wakely, Natural England

Plate 15.6 Lowland acid grassland at Lambert's Castle, Dorset.

variety of topographical situations ranging from level plains such as in the East Anglian Breckland to steep valley slopes. The fine-leaved grasses common bent and sheep's-fescue are almost always present. Typical herbs include sheep's sorrel, tormentil and heath bedstraw.

These grasslands are typically unproductive and are thus most suitable for extensive livestock grazing.

Purple moor-grass and rush pastures

These are sometimes known as marshy grassland and are dominated by purple moor-grass and/or jointed rush species and usually managed as pasture or more rarely as hay meadows. They may also be rich in small sedges. They also support a wide range of herbs characteristic of periodically wet conditions. These include cuckooflower, meadowsweet, ragged-robin, tormentil, devil's-bit scabious, common marsh-bedstraw and greater bird's-foot-trefoil.

These pastures occur mostly on gently sloping ground associated with springs and seepage lines but also occur on river and lake floodplains. They occur on infertile poorly-draining, neutral or mildly acidic peaty mineral soils. These marshy pastures are generally more widespread in western areas of the UK, particularly in Wales, south-west England and Northern Ireland.

Extent and rate of decline in the UK

Lowland semi-natural grasslands sustained severe losses in the second half of the 20th century. For example, it has been estimated that 97% of lowland unimproved grassland was lost between 1930 and 1984 in England and Wales. These losses were largely due to conversion of grassland to arable or intensification by ploughing, drainage and reseeding, improvement with fertilisers and herbicides and a shift from hay to silage. Semi-natural grasslands have also become increasingly fragmented and isolated amongst intensively-managed farmland (see for example Burnside *et al.* 2003).

More recent studies have shown that losses continued in the last two decades of the 20th century. However, there is circumstantial evidence that this decline due to agricultural intensification has recently slowed due to the influence of

Rob Wolton, Natural England

Plate 15.7 Cattle grazing on purple moor-grass and rush pasture.

positive conservation measures and land use regulation.

Conversely, lack of management by grazing or hay cutting, leading to adverse changes in botanical composition, including scrub encroachment, is now increasingly the key issue. This has arisen as a result of specialisation and intensification of the livestock industry resulting in a decline in extensive livestock production and mixed farming systems over the last 50 years.

It is estimated that less than 200, 000 ha of semi-natural grassland now remain in the UK (Table 15.1). This area is only approximately 0.8% of the UK land area.

Table 15.1 Extent of semi-natural lowland grasslands in the UK.

Grassland type	Estimated UK extent in hectares
Lowland meadows and pastures	11,418
Lowland calcareous grassland	40,594
Lowland acid grassland	61,646
Purple moor-grass and rush pastures	79,392
Total	193,050

Source: UK Lowland Grassland Habitat Action Plan Steering Group 2005

Factors affecting status on lowland farmland

Data from various surveillance and monitoring studies provide some insight into the condition of the remaining grassland resource. In a recent sample survey of grassland sites with no statutory protection in England, only 21% were in favourable condition. For grasslands within Sites of Special Scientific Interest (SSSI), the situation is better with an average of 45% favourable and 31% in unfavourable recovering condition.

Much of the resource of lowland semi-natural grassland is still found within privately-owned farmland. In England, for example, around 88% by area of the SSSI estate is not within the ownership of nature conservation bodies (including the National Trust). The equivalent figure for semi-natural grassland (including in this case upland grassland) is 86%. In addition, many nature conservation bodies who own grassland nature reserves rely on farmers entering into agricultural tenancies or short term leases to ensure hay cutting and grazing. In only a relatively few instances are grassland nature reserves directly managed by conservation bodies using their own machinery and livestock.

The remaining resource of lowland semi-natural grassland is now highly fragmented and occurs mostly within a landscape of arable land and intensively managed grassland. Many unimproved neutral meadows and pastures in particular, occur as small, isolated fields often less than 2 ha. These areas are often marginalised and are not seen as an integral part of farm businesses.

However, on a more positive note, there is increasing evidence that the presence of semi-natural grassland and other uncultivated habitats within the farmed landscape may have positive benefits for agricultural crop production. Research has shown that semi-natural grassland can provide a source of insect pollinators for crops such as oil seed rape and thus improve crop production. They may also harbour beneficial invertebrates such as predatory beetles which predate crop pests such as grain aphids.

15.3 Management advice

Maintenance of existing semi-natural grassland

The key to sustaining the wildlife value of most semi-natural grasslands is regular management by cutting and grazing. In the absence of management, the botanical composition will change through the process of succession leading to invasion by woody species and the eventual transformation of grassland into woodland.

For grassland pastures, suitable grazing rates (cattle, sheep and equines) are likely to be between 0.3 and 0.7 LU/ha/year depending on the grassland type. The timing and intensity of grazing will also depend on the specific nature conservation objectives for the site and, inevitably in some cases, on practical considerations such as the availability of suitable livestock.

Hay cutting should take place around early July although an occasional late cut in late July /early August to allow for occasional set seed in late flowering species is probably desirable. Regular late cutting is not advised as it may have detrimental impacts on botanical diversity and produce a crop of lower value to the farmer. Hay meadows should be aftermath grazed to ensure maintenance of botanical diversity. The following provide further guidance on appropriate management treatments

- Avoid the use of inorganic fertilisers or animal slurries as the botanical diversity of semi-natural grasslands will be compromised by increasing the fertility.
- Periodic dressings of farmyard manure are acceptable on meadows as they provide a relatively slow release of nutrients to compensate for the nutrients lost when the hay is harvested. Rates should not exceed 12t/ha/year.
- Mechanical or cultural methods of control of injurious weeds (creeping thistle, spear thistle, broad-leaved and curled dock and common ragwort) or invasive alien species are preferable but if herbicides are needed then targeted methods such as spot treatment and weed wiping should be used.
- Avoid supplementary feeding if possible to avoid poaching and nutrient enrichment of the sward. If necessary, feed in areas of low botanical value.
- Periodic dressings of lime are normally desirable on neutral grasslands.
- Burning of calcareous and purple moor-grass rush pastures may be acceptable in certain circumstances but compliance with grass and heather burning regulations and codes of practice should be ensured.
- Maintain, but do not improve or alter, the existing drainage regime.
- No rolling or harrowing should be practiced between April and early July to protect ground nesting birds.
- When grazing horses and ponies in small pastures, ensure regular collection and removal of dung. Dung removal helps to prevent the establishment of ungrazed latrine areas which are poor in species and often include tall, competitive perennial weeds.

Scrub may be an important component of many semi-natural grasslands. Thus careful management of scrub on grassland sites to maintain wildlife value is a necessary requirement. This can be achieved by a variety of methods including coppicing and livestock grazing.

Creating new grasslands of wildlife value

Ideally, new grassland creation on arable land should be targeted at land with the following characteristics:

- adjacent to existing patches of semi-natural grassland
- low fertility soils ie soil P index of 0 or 1.

The most appropriate method for establishing a new sward will depend on the specific conservation objectives, the nature of the locality, the time scale for establishment and the availability of suitable seed. Natural regeneration will only be suitable on very few sites where the soil fertility is very low, the area is adjacent to existing semi-natural grassland, the field has only recently been converted from semi-natural grassland to arable or contains a range of plants typical of species-rich grassland.

In all other situations, due to seed limitation, swards will need to be established by:

- spreading freshly cut 'green hay' harvested from a nearby semi-natural grassland or
- sowing a seed mix (preferably of locally harvested seed or a bought mixture containing seed of native origin as the next best option)

If using seed, establishment of a diverse sward will normally require the sowing of a species-rich seed mix of species typical of the target grassland type, except in cases where natural regeneration is being facilitated by the sowing of a basic grass seed mix.

Subsequent management will be similar as for existing grasslands. However, regular cutting with removal of the arisings may be required in the first year of management and perennial weed species may be a particular issue that will need addressing.

Diversification of semi-improved, species-poor grassland can be effected by techniques such as over sowing with green hay or a seed mix following scarification by chain harrowing, slot seeding or the introduction of pot-grown or seedling plugs of wildflowers.

Case study of best practice management: Applesham Farm, West Sussex

Applesham Farm near East Lancing, West Sussex is situated in the South Downs Area of Outstanding Natural Beauty (AONB) and the South Downs Environmentally Sensitive Area (ESA). It is farmed by Chris Passmore who is the third generation of his family to farm the land. It comprises mostly rolling chalk downland and is situated on chalky loam soils. The farm is a mixed enterprise of around 344 ha comprising sheep (400 breeding ewes), beef suckler cattle (100-head) and grain production. The livestock and arable enterprises are fully integrated with a rotation that allows three years of cereals followed by three years of grass/clover leys. Crops of mustard, forage rape and Italian rye-grass are slotted in where possible to provide additional livestock grazing. Cereal stubbles are grazed before being ploughed up to grow the following year's crop.

An existing area of 28 ha of calcareous grassland on steep slopes was entered into the ESA scheme (now replaced by the Environmental Stewardship Scheme). This provides incentive payments in return for environmentally sensitive management. The bank is grazed year round when adjoining fields are down to leys for a period of three years with no inputs of fertiliser. When the adjoining fields are growing cereals, the bank is grazed briefly between harvest and autumn ploughing.

In addition, about 35 ha of steeper, less fertile arable land has been converted into grassland with a view to establishing a sward similar to chalk grassland. This area is grazed by sheep and cattle. The extensive management of the land entered into the ESA scheme covering about one fifth of the farm relies on the yield achieved by other land on the rest of the farm. For example, to provide sufficient winter feed and bedding straw for livestock, to allow movement of livestock from the scheme areas to meet conservation objectives, or to allow for a variable stocking rate to reflect seasonal herbage growth.

The tall, uncropped, grassland along fence-lines and farm lanes provides reservoirs of predatory invertebrates which feed on grain aphids. These are usually sufficient to keep aphid numbers below the economic threshold for crop spraying.

Further reading

Borges C and Rotheroe M (2002) Managing land with fungi in mind. *Enact* 10 (3): 17–22.

Britt C, Mole A, Kirkham F and Terry A (2003) *The herbicide handbook: guidance on the use of herbicides on nature conservation sites*. FACT/English Nature, Peterborough.

Burnside N G, Smith R F and Waite S (2003) Recent historical land use change on the South Downs, United Kingdom. *Environmental Conservation* 30: 52–60.

Crofts A and Jefferson R G (1999) *The lowland grassland management handbook*. English Nature/The Wildlife Trusts, Peterborough.

Day J, Symes N and Robertson P (2003) *The scrub management handbook: guidance on the management of scrub on nature conservation sites*. FACT/English Nature, Peterborough.

Flora Locale (2005) *Go native! Planting for biodiversity: guidelines for planting projects in the countryside: promoting the wise use and supply of native flora*. Flora locale, Hungerford. [http://www.floralocale.org/]

Fuller R M (1987) The changing extent and conservation interest of lowland grasslands in England and Wales: a review of grassland surveys 1930–1984. *Biological Conservation* 40: 281–300.

Hewins E J, Pinches C, Arnold J, Lush M, Robertson H and Escott S (2005) The condition of lowland BAP priority grasslands: results from a sample survey of non-statutory stands in England. *English Nature Research Reports,* No 636. Peterborough: English Nature.

Jefferson R G (2007) Grassland ecosystem services: can they help the case for conservation? *In*: J J Hopkins (ed.) *High value grassland: providing biodiversity, a clean environment and premium products.* British Grassland Society Occasional Symposium No. 38. Cirencester: British Grassland Society.

Passmore C W (1997) Farming in the South Downs. *In*: R D Sheldrick (ed) *Grassland management in the Environmentally Sensitive Areas.* British Grassland Society Occasional Symposium No. 32 Reading: British Grassland Society, pp128–131.

Pinches C and Rimes C (2007) The state of species-rich lowland grassland in the UK: problems at the grass roots. *In*: J J Hopkins (ed.) *High value grassland: providing biodiversity, a clean environment and premium products.* British Grassland Society Occasional Symposium No. 38. Cirencester: British Grassland Society.

Robertson H J and Jefferson R G (2000) Monitoring the condition of lowland grassland SSSIs. Volume I: English Nature's rapid assessment system. *English Nature Research Reports*, No 315. English Nature, Peterborough.

Rodwell J S (ed.) (1991) *British plant communities 2: Mires and heaths.* Cambridge: Cambridge University Press.

Rodwell J S (ed.) (1992) *British plant communities 3: Grassland and montane communities.* Cambridge University Press, Cambridge.

Rural Development Service (2003) Arable reversion to species-rich grassland: site selection and choice of methods. *Technical Advice Note* 21. [http://www.defra.gov.uk/rds/publications/technical/tan_21.pdf]

Rural Development Service (2004) Arable reversion to species-rich grassland: establishment of a sown sward. *Technical Advice Note* 24. [http://www.defra.gov.uk/rds/publications/technical/tan_24.pdf

Rural Development Service (2004) Arable reversion to species-rich grassland: early management of the new sward. *Technical Advice Note* 25. [http://www.defra.gov.uk/rds/publications/technical/tan_25.pdf]

Rural Development Service (2004) Sward enhancement: Selection of suitable sites. *Technical Advice Note* 26. [http://www.defra.gov.uk/rds/publications/technical/tan_26.pdf]

Rural Development Service (2004) Sward enhancement: diversifying grassland using pot grown wildflowers or seedling plugs. *Technical Advice Note* 30. [http://www.defra.gov.uk/rds/publications/technical/tan_30.pdf]

Index

Notes: *Italic* page numbers refer to photographs and **bold** numbers refer to figures and tables.

Species index

Notes: *Italic* page numbers refer to photographs and **bold** numbers refer to figures and tables.